THE BATTLE OF HEXHAM
IN ITS PLACE

JOHN SADLER AND ALEX SPEIRS

ERGO PRESS

Publishing for Northumberland

THE BATTLE OF HEXHAM
IN ITS PLACE

First published 2007
by Ergo Press

Illustrations by Chloe Rodham © Ergo Press
Cover graphics by Slim Palmer
Photographs by Alan Isaac Grint

ISBN -13: 978-0-9552758-7-6
ISBN -10: 0-9552758-7-3

ERGO PRESS
5, St Mary's Chare
Hexham
Northumberland
NE46 1NQ
www.ergopress.com
ergo.press@yahoo.co.uk

ABOUT THE AUTHORS

John Sadler is a Fellow of the Royal Historical Society and of the Society of Antiquaries of Scotland. A military historian working in mid-Northumberland, he is married with two teenage daughters. He has published extensively on the border wars and the border reivers and his military history of the Wars of the Roses will be published by Longmans in 2008. Visit www.johnsadler.net

Alex Speirs read Archaeology at Liverpool University before entering museum education, working in a number of venues across the north east of England for several years. She now works as a freelance museum educationalist, passionate about sharing her love of history with other people. This is her first formal attempt to do this using the written word.

ACKNOWLEDGEMENTS

The authors would like to thank Julia Grint for her editorial work and Alan Grint for his photographs. The maps and genealogical tables were drawn by Slim Palmer and the original line drawings by Chloe Rodham.

TABLE OF CONTENTS

Dramatis Personae
The major characters in this account

Genealogical Tables
The Houses of Lancaster and York

Part One: Being Introductory   Page 1
Wars of the Roses · background

Part Two: The Wars of the Roses as History   Page 7
The Wars as perceived by contemporary chroniclers and by historians
from Tudor times onwards.

Part Three: The Art of War in the Fifteenth Century   Page 13
The art of war in the late medieval period · chivalry · weaponry · castles and
sieges · naval architecture · strategy and tactics · livery and maintenance ·
combat · wounds and medical services · logistics.

Part Four: The French Wars and the House of Lancaster   Page 43
The French Wars as backdrop to the Wars of the Roses · the Lancastrian
usurpation.

Part Five: The Unquiet Peace   Page 69
The Percy v Neville feud · mental breakdown of Henry VI and birth of his
son · York becomes Protector · Battles of 1st St Albans, Blore Heath, Rout
of Ludford Bridge, Northampton, Wakefield, 2nd St Albans, Mortimer's
Cross and Towton · Edward Earl of March recognised as Edward IV by
Warwick 'The Kingmaker'.

Part Six: The War in the North   Page 91

The cockpit of war moves northwards into Northumberland · state of the Border · the castles of Northumberland · Queen Margaret in Scotland · Yorkists v Lancastrians in Northumberland · Queen Margaret in France.

Part Seven: Hedgeley Moor and Hexham 1464   Page 111

Edward IV attempts conciliation with Somerset (failed) · Henry VI has 'court' in Bamburgh · Battle of Hedgeley Moor and death of Ralph Percy · Henry VI at Bywell in Tynedale · the Battle of Hexham · executions in the Market Place · capitulation of castles of Alnwick and Dunstanburgh; artillery bombardment of Bamburgh · end of War in the North.

Part Eight: The Legacy   Page 141

Edward IV marries Elizabeth Woodville · Warwick and Clarence · 'Lose-cote Field' · Warwick allies with Margaret of Anjou and invades England · Edward IV flees to France · Re-adeption of Henry VI · Battle of Barnet and death of Warwick · Battle of Tewkesbury and death of Prince Edward of Lancaster · murder of Henry VI in Tower · Death of Edward IV · Richard of Gloucester usurps the crown as Richard III · Defeat and death of Richard at Bosworth · Henry VII becomes first Tudor king.

Part Nine: The Battlefield Tour   Page 145

Guided tour of the major sites mentioned in this book.

Timeline   Page 153

Glossary   Page 155

Bibliography and Sources   Page 161

DRAMATIS PERSONAE

George, Duke of Clarence (1449-1478)
'False, perjured Clarence', younger brother of Edward IV and Warwick's co-conspirator in 1469-1470. When Warwick reached his accord with Margaret of Anjou, his new son in law (Clarence) proved a pretender too many and Clarence reverted to his brother's side (Edward IV) for the campaigns of Barnet and Tewkesbury, his inveterate plotting and the enmity of the Woodville brood, hastened his fall.

John Beaufort, 1st Duke of Somerset (1403-1444)
John was the second son of John Beaufort, 1st Earl of Somerset. He suceeded his older brother Henry as 3rd Earl of Somerset in 1418. He was taken in the rout at Beauge and imprisoned for seventeen years, before being ransomed. He was elevated to the dukedom in1443, a year before his death, which may have been suicide.

Edmund Beaufort, 2nd Duke of Somerset (1406-1455)
Edmund succeeded his brother John on his death in 1444, like John he had been captured at Beauge and remained a prisoner until 1427. Since the title was recreated after his brother's death, he was technically still the first Duke, although he styled himself the second. Though head of a great family his income was modest, far below that of his rival York; although he became a key Lancastrian figure, his career was distinguished by venality and military failure. Generally detested, he fell at 1st St Albans.

Henry Beaufort, 3rd Duke of Somerset (1436-1464)
Eldest son of Edmund, he was wounded at 1st St Albans, where his father fell. A prime mover in the Lancastrian revival after the constitutional settlement of 1460, he fought at Wakefield and 2nd St Albans, where his

generalship proved superior. Defeated at Towton, he maintained the war in the north and though he capitulated in 1463, he reverted the following year and was executed after the débâcle at Hexham.

Edmund Beaufort, titular 4th Duke of Somerset (1438-1471)

Younger brother of the 3rd Duke, led the Lancastrians in the campaign and battle of Tewkesbury, taken from sanctuary and beheaded the day after the defeat.

John de Clifford, 13th Baron Clifford (1435-1461)

Member of a long established family with extensive lands in the north-west. After his father was killed at the 1st Battle of St Albans, 'Butcher Clifford' became a savage paladin of the House of Lancaster. He fought at Wakefield and is credited with the slaying of Edmund, Earl of Rutland, second son of Richard, Duke of York. He was, in turn, killed in the skirmish at Dintingdale prior to the Battle of Towton and his followers, 'The Flower of Craven' were slain around him.

Thomas Grey, Marquess of Dorset (1451-1501)

Elizabeth Woodville's son by her first (Lancastrian) husband, remained loyal to Edward IV. He competed with Lord Hastings for the affections of a number of mistresses, including the celebrated Jane Shore. After the usurpation of Richard III he fled to join Henry Tudor, but his loyalty was never certain.

Henry VI of England (1422-1471)

Pious but ineffectual, he married Margaret of Anjou in 1445. Prone to bouts of insanity, frequently a mere pawn in the game of state, he was finally done to death in the Tower after his son and heir, Edward of Lancaster, was killed at Tewkesbury.

Henry VII of England (1457-1509)

Son of Edmund Tudor, Earl of Richmond, and Lady Margaret Beaufort, nephew to Jasper Tudor, Earl of Pembroke, a leading Welsh Lancastrian. His claim to inherit the mantle of the House of Lancaster was more expedient than real.

Henry Holand, 3rd Duke of Exeter (d.1475)

A particularly thuggish example of a magnatial bully. Despite his wedding to one of York's daughters he came to be implicated in the disturbances of 1453 as a partisan of the Percies. He fought at Blore Heath, Wakefield, 2nd St Albans, Towton and Barnet, where he was left for dead on the field but escaped (his Yorkist wife had abandoned him, some time before!) He escaped to the continent, where he was reduced to beggary though he met his end as a prisoner in the Tower, in dubious circumstances.

Edward of Lancaster (1453-1471)

Only child of Henry VI and Margaret of Anjou (some questions were raised as to his legitimacy), he was raised in exile in readiness for an attempt to recover his father's throne. Allied to the Kingmaker, by marriage to a younger daughter, his chance came and went, together with his life, at Tewkesbury

Edward, Earl of March (1442-1483)

King of England 1461-1470 and 1471-1483. 'The Sunne in Splendour', he was the eldest son of the Duke of York and Cicely Neville, 'The Rose of Raby'. He married Elizabeth Woodville.

Margaret of Anjou (d.1482)

As Queen, and with her favourite the Duke of Somerset, she dominated the Lancastrian court faction and, until 1463, was the mainspring of resistance in the north, where she had been prepared to swap the twin bastions of Berwick upon Tweed and Carlisle in return for Scottish arms. A daughter of René, King of Naples and Duke of Bar, she was kept in the Tower after the disaster at Tewkesbury until finally being released in 1475. She spent her final years in Anjou.

Richard Neville, Earl of Salisbury (1400-1460)
Younger son of the Earl of Westmorland, he received the lesser share of the family estates on the east side. In addition to his feud with the Percies he was at odds with the senior branch of the Nevilles. Brother in law to the Duke of York, he was active in Yorkist councils and a senior statesman in the cause, killed after Wakefield with one of his sons Sir Thomas Neville, whose marriage to Maud Stanhope fanned the flames of the Percy/Neville feud.

William Neville, Lord Fauconberg (c1410-1463)
Younger son of Ralph, Earl of Westmorland, brother of the Earl of Salisbury, and a veteran of the French Wars. He successfully led the Yorkist van at Northampton and Towton, acquired his title by right of his wife, (who lacked mental capacity).

Thomas Neville, 'Bastard' of Fauconberg (d.1471)
Something of a swashbuckler and buccaneer, he was active on the Lancastrian side in 1471 and, though pardoned, suffered execution later in that year.

Richard Neville, Earl of Warwick (1428-1471)
Known as 'The Kingmaker', mightiest of the over-mighty subjects and a pivotal figure in the period. He was Salisbury's eldest son and York's nephew, married a daughter of Richard Beauchamp Earl of Warwick. He

fought at 1st St Albans, Northampton, 2nd St Albans and Towton. Seeing himself as the power behind the throne, he was increasingly alienated from Edward IV following the Woodville marriage. His final manipulation led to the 'Re-adeption' of Henry VI in the coup of 1470. He was killed at Barnet with his brother, Lord Montagu.

John Neville, Lord Montagu (d.1471)

The Earl of Warwick's younger brother, an able soldier and administrator, principal architect of the Yorkist victory in the north from 1461 – 1464. Temporarily installed as Earl of Northumberland, he was later stripped of the title and though partly compensated, joined his brother in the coup of 1470, dying with him at Barnet.

Thomas Percy, Lord Egremont (1422-1460)

Younger son of the 2nd Earl of Northumberland, created Lord Egremont in 1445, violent and thuggish, an actor in the Percy/Neville feud on the early 1450s. He was killed at Northampton.

Henry Percy, 2nd Earl of Northumberland (d.1455)

Son of the famous Henry Percy 'Hotspur', killed at Shrewsbury in 1403. He gradually clawed back the family lands after his father's attainder, was involved in the rivalry with the Nevilles and was killed at 1st St Albans.

Henry Percy, Lord Poynings, later 3rd Earl of Northumberland (d.1461)

Border Warden after his father, he was one of the leading northern Lancastrians, fighting at Wakefield, 2nd St Albans and Towton, where he fell. The title was, once again, attainted after his death, passing to John Neville, Lord Montagu. Edward IV subsequently restored his son, who became the 4th Earl. A far more slippery character than his father and determined to be on the winning side. He appeared to work well with

Richard III as Duke of Gloucester from 1471-1483, though his role at Bosworth was ambivalent. He flourished briefly under Henry VII but was murdered by a mob of rioters in York.

Sir Ralph Percy (d.1464)
Margaret of Anjou's champion in the North 1461-1464. Though prone to switching allegiance, he reverted to Lancaster for the last time before the rout at Hedgeley Moor, where he was slain.

Henry Stafford, 2nd Duke of Buckingham (1454-1483)
Married against his will to one of Elizabeth Woodville's seemingly endless line of sisters, he became a prime mover in the counsels of the Duke of Gloucester leading up to and during the usurpation. Disappointed, he later rebelled, a still-born affair which lead to his execution.

Thomas, Lord Stanley, Earl of Derby (1435-1504)
Fourth husband of Margaret Beaufort and a leading magnate in the North West, he at first served but, at Bosworth, betrayed Richard III, his intervention being decisive in the King's defeat, a defection which earned him a peerage.

John Tiptoft, Earl of Worcester (1427-1470)
Held the office of Constable of England 1462-1467 and again in 1470. Noted both for his extensive literary tastes, his outstanding library and his ferocious cruelty. A devotee of anal impalement as a mode of execution, he was universally reviled and Warwick had him executed in 1470, primarily as a sop to widespread clamour.

Sir Andrew Trollope (d.1461)
Successful soldier who fought in the French Wars and acted, first, as

an advisor to York, his defection provoking the collapse of morale and subsequent 'Rout' of Ludford. He may have been instrumental in the Lancastrians' winning tactics at Wakefield and fought with distinction at 2nd St Albans. His luck finally ran out at Towton.

Edmund Tudor, Earl of Richmond (1430-1456)

The son of Own Tudor (d.1461, executed after Mortimer's Cross), and Katherine of Valois, widow of Henry V, he married the formidable Margaret Beaufort and fathered Henry Tudor, the future Henry VII, before succumbing to a bout of the plague.

Jasper Tudor, Earl of Pembroke (1431-1495)

Brother of Edmund, a diehard Lancastrian, he fought at 1st St Albans, Mortimer's Cross and Towton, an unfortunate combination of engagements. After an unsuccessful attempt to relieve Harlech, he fled in 1468 to Brittany. He at last fought for a winning side at Bosworth and subsequently married Buckingham's Woodville widow.

Queen Elizabeth Woodville (1437-1492)

Married to the Lancastrian knight Sir John Grey of Groby, and then widowed. Edward IV married her in secret to the great consternation of his supporters, most particularly Warwick, who had been seeking to broker a French alliance. Noted for her ruthless avarice and rapacity, her family were excoriated for their shameless greed.

Richard Woodville 1st Earl Rivers (d.1469)

Elizabeth's father, married to Jacquetta of Luxembourg, widow of the Earl of Bedford, Henry V's brother, and regent after his death. Initially an adherent of Lancaster, fighting at Towton, he held high office under his son in law, earning the powerful enmity of the Earl of Warwick, who had him executed after the defeat at Edgecote.

Elizabeth of York (1466-1503)

Eldest daughter of Edward IV and Elizabeth Woodville, possibly pursued by her uncle Richard III after his widowhood, she eventually married Henry Tudor, thus effecting the symbolic union of Lancaster and York.

Margaret of York, Duchess of Burgundy (1446-1503)

Sister of Edward IV she was married to the mercurial and quixotic Charles the Bold, Duke of Burgundy (d.1477). She remained a Yorkist plotter and intermeddler after the death of her brother at Bosworth.

Richard, Duke of York (c.1410-1460)

The senior member of the Yorkist faction, with a strong claim to the throne, active in the later stages of the French wars, a bitter opponent of Somerset, Lord Protector on two occasions, claimed the throne in 1460 and was killed at Wakefield at the end of that year.

TABLE A: THE HOUSE OF YORK

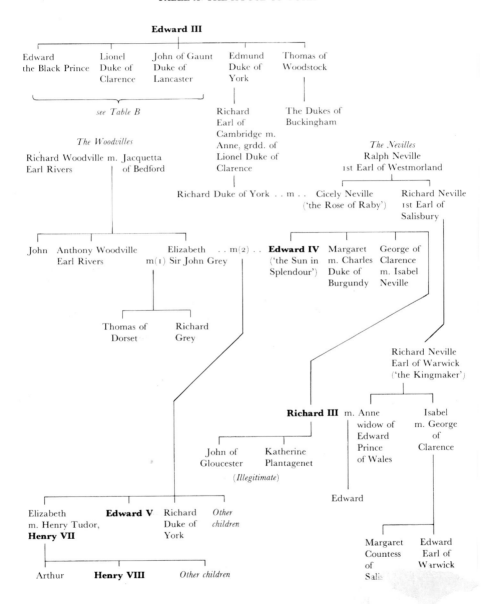

TABLE B: THE HOUSES OF LANCASTER AND TUDOR

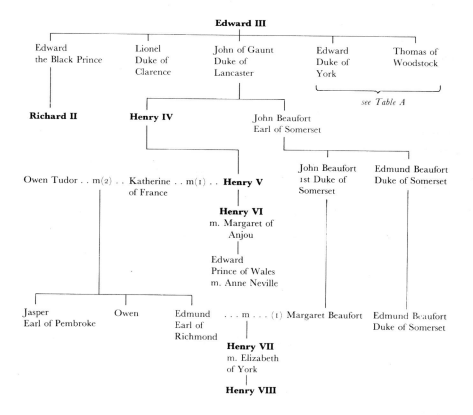

PART ONE

BEING INTRODUCTORY

On a late summer's day in August 1485, a slightly built, dark-haired man observed from horseback the action of the Battle of Bosworth Field as it was played out. This was Richard III, King of England, and this day he would die in battle – the last English monarch to do so. The King's van was in disarray, his loyal subordinate Lord John Howard, Duke of Norfolk, lay dead. Henry Percy, 4th Earl of Northumberland, who had sworn allegiance to the king, remained in the rear of Richard's army, artfully motionless.

Fuelled by desperation, King Richard launched a direct assault on the Pretender, Henry Tudor, and his meagre bodyguard. Shakespeare has him exhorting his followers:

> *Go, gentlemen, every man unto his charge:*
> *Let not our babbling dreams affright our souls;*
> *Conscience is but a word that cowards use,*
> *Devised at first to keep the strong in awe:*
> *Our strong arms be our conscience, swords our law.*
> *March on, join bravely, let us to't pell-mell;*
> *If not to heaven, then hand in hand to hell.*

Richard III, Act V, Sc iv

Tactically, this could just have been a masterstroke; the Stanleys, who had been waiting on the side lines, clearly thought so and judged this to be the moment to come 'off the fence' and commit themselves to Henry Tudor. Richard was unhorsed, crying out repeatedly against 'treason' whilst wielding his war hammer to deadly effect. He was finally cut down by the slashing blades around him, royal blood mingling with the mud of the field.

CR

Richard III
1452-1485

Richard's body was stripped naked and slung over a horse to be paraded as a trophy before the commoners, and as the parade made its way into nearby Leicester his corpse jogged like a broken marionette. Finally, his broken remains were flung, unceremoniously, into a dry water trough – a humiliating end for the last Plantagenet King of England.

Such images have frequently been employed in describing the final dramatic act of the period of civil strife labelled the 'Wars of the Roses'. These 'wars' were a series of battles, skirmishes and sieges that took place between 1453 and 1487. The quarrel mainly involved the great magnates of England, who owned great swathes of land and property with their titles. The lower orders – as their supporters, tenants and, in the case of the military contract system, their retainers – were also involved.

The cause of the Wars of the Roses was a dynastic dispute, the prize for the victor was the throne of England. In the 14th Century, King Edward III was blessed with five sons, thereby creating a complicated and extended family tree. In the 1450s, some eighty years after his death, two different branches of this tree asserted their right to rule England. These branches were known as the 'House of Lancaster' and the 'House of York', along with their 'affinity' (their retainers and supporters) who were known as 'Lancastrians' and 'Yorkists'.

The Wars of the Roses was not a name given to the conflict at the time. The term was possibly coined in the 19th Century by Sir Walter Scott, whose dramatic flair was never clouded by too much factual analysis! The 'Roses' in question were the white rose of York and the red rose of Lancaster – the supposed emblems of the two different houses. In the 15th Century every great lord and those connected to him sported an emblem that easily identified them. Edward IV wore the 'sunne in splendour' for example. 'Lancaster' and 'York' never uniformly adopted the rose as their defining emblems, but it is possible that the Beaufort family, Dukes of Somerset and Lancastrian in sentiment, adopted the red rose. It also seems that the Mortimer family, Earls of March and Yorkist in affinity, wore a white rose. Elizabeth of York also adopted the white rose. Henry Tudor, the Lancastrian Pretender to the throne, took the red rose as his emblem, to which he had a right via his mother, Margaret Beaufort. When he married Elizabeth in 1486 the two roses were combined to make the red and white 'Tudor Rose'.

For the purposes of this narrative, the actual events of the Wars of the Roses have been broken up into five distinct sections. Although the people involved in the wars would probably not have classified the action so neatly, it is useful for the reader to see at a glance how the wars took their course:

Period One: 1450 – 1455

The breakdown of the administration of Henry VI, the end of the French Wars and the English defeat, the emergence of the Percy v Neville feud and events leading up to the campaign and Battle of 1st St Albans.

Period Two: 1459 – 1461

The outbreak of enmity that led firstly to Blore Heath and the Rout of Ludford Bridge and then the battles of Northampton, Wakefield, Mortimer's Cross, 2nd St Albans and Towton.

Period Three: 1461 – 1464

The 'outpost' war, fought mainly in north-east England and Wales, including the Battles of Hedgeley Moor and Hexham.

Period Four: 1468 – 1471

The disturbances orchestrated by Richard Neville, Earl of Warwick; the battles of Edgecote and Empingham; the 'Readeption' (restoration to the throne) of Henry VI and the battles of Barnet and Tewkesbury. The climax of these battles saw the demise of the Nevilles and the extinction of the old Lancastrian Line, with the Yorkist ascendancy apparently firmly established.

Period Five: 1483 – 1487

This represents the contest between York, in the person of the usurper Richard III, and Henry Tudor as ostensible champion of the rump of the Lancastrian affinity; the Battle of Bosworth.

This book aims to give the reader an overview of this exciting and intriguing period of history by focussing on the politics and military action of the time. The Wars of the Roses involved many different characters, all of them with a family name and most with a title. More often than not the book will refer to the major players by their title, so Richard Neville, Earl of Warwick will often be referred to as 'Warwick', his father Richard Neville Earl of Salisbury will be referred to as 'Salisbury' and so on. The full name of an individual will be used intermittently to make matters clear.

The book also touches upon the interpretation of the Wars of the Roses in history and takes a closer look at 15th Century warfare. There is an emphasis on the events that took place before the outbreak of war – dynastic struggles in England and the Hundred Years War in France – which undoubtedly set the events of the Wars of the Roses in motion. Finally, the book aims to bring the reader a detailed account of the War in the North. Although the first phase of the conflict took place in Yorkshire, the action then moved, for the most part, to Northumberland; the existing situation in this most northerly of shires made for a very different type of warfare. The book also touches specifically upon a battle of real local interest – the Battle of Hexham in 1464. This was a small skirmish which nevertheless had a great impact as it signalled the end for Henry Beaufort, 3rd Duke of Somerset – a major player in the wars. If one considers the numbers of men involved and the casualties that resulted, the Battle of Hexham cannot be compared with Towton, or indeed with any of the other major battles: Hexham was more of a rout than a slogging match and probably more men died in the rash of executions that followed than were killed on the field. Nonetheless, it was strategically decisive in the history of the War in the North, bringing to a conclusion three years of sieges, marches, counter-marches and battles. The Battle of Hexham has never been fully narrated, unlike other, major battles. There is no marker to commemorate the fight and, significantly, most writers have placed the action in an incorrect location.

CR

Elizabeth Woodville
1466-1503

In victory, Henry went on to make the excellent political move of marrying Elizabeth Woodville or 'Elizabeth of York', daughter of the previous Yorkist King, Edward IV, who died in 1483 from natural causes. By marrying Elizabeth, Henry united the houses of Lancaster and York. The final Yorkist challenge of the Wars of the Roses came at the Battle of Stoke in 1487. The army of King Henry VII triumphed over the forces of the imposter Lambert Simnel backed by the powerful Earl of Lincoln.

Despite being fearful of rebellion and usurpation for most of his reign, Henry passed the crown safely to his own son, Henry VIII, when he died in 1509. In the 16th Century, the houses of Lancaster and York faded into memory and the 'House of Tudor' prevailed.

PART TWO

THE WARS OF THE ROSES AS HISTORY

The Wars of the Roses as an *idea*, as an impression – handed down to us through the centuries by scholars and historians – is generally a very unpleasant one. The prevailing attitude for many years has been that the wars were basically 'gang warfare' – a collection of clannish 'robber barons' spilling each other's blood with reckless enthusiasm. One is led to assume that such destructive behaviour must have been detrimental to England as a whole. As Pollard points out in his book on late medieval England, the Wars of the Roses have become a paradigm for misrule, violence and anarchy.

Edward IV, the Yorkist King who ruled from 1461-1483 (with a brief interruption during the 'Re-adeption' of Henry VI, 1470-1471) employed the argument that the conflicts of the age were God's verdict on the Lancastrian usurpation of 1399, a progressive working out of divine wrath. God's anger was only assuaged when he, Edward, acceded to the throne and restored the natural order. So was born a powerful piece of propaganda whereby the Wars of the Roses were seen as civil unrest that could only be remedied by the enthroning of a rightful king, elected by God. Henry Tudor, too, leapt onto this particular bandwagon when he became Henry VII, and before him the usurper Richard III employed the very same tack when he hurried to stress the uncertainties of his late brother's reign in a declamation to Parliament. He also stressed how every person in England felt the effects of his brother's unlawful rule:

> [N]o man was sure of his life, land, nor livelihood, nor of his wife, daughter, nor servant, every good maiden and woman standing to dread to be ravished and befouled. And besides this, what discords, inward battles, effusion of Christian men's blood, and namely by the destruction of the noble blood of this land, was had and committed within the same, it is evident and notorious through all this realm, unto the great sorrow and heaviness of all true Englishmen.[1]

Tudor chroniclers, beginning with Polydore Virgil in the time of Henry VII, followed by Edward Hall, Sir Thomas Smith and William Shakespeare, moulded this crude propaganda into historical doctrine. They asserted that the origins of the conflict lay in the usurpation of 1399, when Henry Bolingbroke (Henry IV) took the throne from his cousin Richard II. The dire working out of this abomination encompassed both the magnates and the commons, a judgement upon England.

Edward Hall also distinguished between the regular perils of factionalism (the rivalry between baronial affinities often revolving around land and property disputes) and the far more calamitous division between Lancaster and York, which split the realm in two. The theme, enthusiastically taken up by Sir Thomas Smith, was one of chaos: an unravelling of the nation, washed down with gallons of gore. He implied that the wars were no mere baronial brawl but were a deep-rooted conflict that blighted the whole of late medieval society.

The imagery was perfected by the dramatist's pen of William Shakespeare, with his masterful additional flourishes. His cycle of history plays: Henry IV Parts 1 and 2, Henry V, Henry VI Parts 1, 2, and 3, and Richard III, exposed the woes that arise when lawful and divinely ordained authority is overthrown. This message is most forcefully driven home in the character of Richard III, the archetypical villain: cynical, murderous and unfit for kingship. Modern historians are fairly evenly divided as to whether this is an accurate portrayal.

As Pollard points out, a further influence which helped to define the Wars of the Roses as lawless and chaotic was the *Humanist* ideal that took root during the 16th Century. *Renaissance Humanism* sought to rediscover and re-translate early versions of the Bible and the works of the great writers of ancient Greece and Rome in the hope of using the knowledge found therein to create a world where people lived good, educated Christian lives. The time between the ancient Classical world and this new enlightened era was deemed to be a period of uncouth and uncongenial behaviour, orchestrated by a cadre of thuggish lords.

During the 19th Century, when antiquarianism flourished in the glow of imperial riches, history came of age as a serious discipline. The view of the Wars of the Roses as a lawless, corrupt affair, orchestrated by a class of over-mighty subjects, held sway. The moralistic tone of 19th Century writers such as William Denton [2] recoiled at this picture of amoral, anarchistic chaos, which was the antithesis of the contemporary Whiggish disciplines of Capitalism and Reason.

In the 20th Century, this theory finally began to be called into question. Green, in his *Short History of the English People*, advanced the view that the discord was mainly confined to the magnates and their coteries and that the mercantile and artisan classes were relatively unaffected. This argument was considerably advanced by Kingsford who laid stress on the positive aspects of the late 15th Century, which witnessed growing cultural and economic development in both town and shire.

Kingsford's successors refined this view still further with the emerging argument that the late 15th Century was no more lawless or corrupt than had been preceding eras, and that the politics of affinity and patronage were by no means unique to the period. K.B. MacFarlane stressed the limited nature of military conflict and saw the prime cause of discord as the weakness of Henry VI and his administration. The whole theory of divine working began to unravel.

Two of the most influential modern historians, J.R. Lander and C. Ross, have concluded that the effects of the conflict were limited. They assert that little or no large scale devastation and social disruption ensued and that the burgeoning cultural development of England was neither curtailed nor inhibited. J. Gillingham, writing as recently as 1981, took the view that 15th Century England was a model of peace and order compared to the state of her European neighbours; a comparable study of Scotland during the period would reveal a considerably less ordered society in

James III of Scotland
1451-1488

which MacDonald Lords of the Isles threatened internal calm [3]. As for the Kings of Scotland – of the first four James, the first [4] and the third were murdered [5], the second died of wounds [6] and the fourth was killed in battle against the English [7]. This is not to assert that life in England during the latter half of the 15th Century was idyllic – very far from it; any breakdown of central authority provided scope for local magnates to resolve their differences with the sword. However, a broad look at society and economic development does suggest that the country experienced flourishing trade and cultural growth that continued at an increasing pace, as though the land were entirely at peace. Even the medieval castle, perhaps the most potent and enduring symbol of warfare, was going out of vogue – at least in its purely defensive form [8] and Caxton introduced the printing press into England [9].

There is, furthermore, a realisation that the effects of conflict were felt in different ways depending on locality. It could be argued, for instance, that the wars in Northumberland between 1461 and 1464 had an entirely different effect upon that county than the previous episodes had upon North Yorkshire. For Northumberland it could be said that strife was simply 'business as usual' in an area where war and raiding against the Scots were the norm.

It is now generally accepted that the late 15th Century was neither more nor less moral than any other time, and that the *idea* of the Wars of the Roses was more horrific to the early historians than were the possible widespread effects. Fighting over who should be King, a position which in theory should be chosen by God, was deeply disturbing to the English psyche; the actual accompanying warfare was not (at least amongst the ruling classes!) viewed with the same sense of horror, since the social mores of the time made the pursuit of glory in battle a noble pursuit rather than a tragic waste of human life.

Notes:

[1] Pollard A J, *'The Wars of the Roses'* London 1998 p.8

[2] Pollard op. cit. p.12

[3] The chiefs of Clan Donald had existed in semi-independence since the 12th Century as Lords of the Isles, holding sway over the majority of the Norse-Gael clans of the Western Highlands and Islands. In 1411, as a result of a feudal dispute, they had clashed with the Earl of Mar, the crown's representative in the North-East at Harlaw by Inverurie, and a savage and prolonged conflict ensued – one of the bloodiest fields in Scottish medieval history. James IV finally abolished the title, by then moribund, in 1493.

[4] James I was murdered in 1436 by disaffected nobles.

[5] James III was killed in the aftermath of his defeat by his magnatial opponents at Sauchieburn in 1488. The same faction had orchestrated a mass cull of the King's unpopular and base-born favourites during Gloucester's campaign of 1482

[6] James II was killed when one of his pieces of ordnance burst at the siege of Roxburgh. For much of his reign he had been at odds with the powerful affinity of the Black Douglas.

[7] James IV died at Flodden in 1513.

[8] Good examples are Bodiam and Herstmonceux, both in East Sussex,

[9] The first Humanist Grammar School, Magdalen College School, Oxford, was founded during the period, see Pollard op. cit. p.3

PART THREE

THE ART OF WAR

IN THE FIFTEENTH CENTURY

'The blood of English shall manure the ground,
And future ages groan for this foul act;
Peace shall go to sleep with Turks and infidels,
And, in this seat of peace, tumultuous wars,
Shall kin with kin, and kind with kind confound;
Disorder, Horror, Fear and Mutiny
Shall here inhabit, and this land be call'd
The field of Golgotha and dead men's skulls.

'Collectarium Mansuetudinum et Bonorum Morum Regis Henrici VI, ex Collectione Magistri Joannis Blakman bacchalaurei theologiae, et post Cartusiae monachi Londoni' ed. and trans. M.R. James as 'Henry Sixth'.

During the Wars of the Roses, the main protagonists were of noble birth and rode on horseback in full plate armour, being 'horsed and harnessed' (although they actually fought on foot for the better part of a mêlée).   In the 15th Century it was still common for Commanders-in-Chief to be present on the battlefield and to engage in hand to hand combat if the need arose.

The profession of arms was one of only a handful of 'career options' open to a man of good family, and he would train assiduously from an early age. As a boy he would generally be placed in the house of another noble to receive training amongst his peers, and as a squire he would remain a trainee until being knighted, which would take several years. New knights were often dubbed on the eve of battle or in the aftermath, having distinguished themselves in the fight. In Shakespeare's Henry V, in the aftermath of the battle, the victorious King Henry mentions that of those Frenchman who died on the field of Agincourt, many were nobles, 'of the which five hundred were but yesterday dubb'd knights' (Act IV, sc.viii).

Poleaxe

The romantic image of mounted knight carrying sword, shield and lance was not a reality at this time; rather, he fought with a variety of gruesome implements, astonishingly effective in trained hands; a gentleman's choice of weapon depended on personal preference, skill and wealth. One of the most popular weapons, for example, was not the heroic sword but the fearsome poleaxe: a heavy axe blade on a stout ash shaft from 4' to 6' in length (1.2m to 1.8m). A hefty 'beak' or hammer head was on the reverse of the blade and the head tapered to a wicked spike. This tool was designed to defeat the armourer's art by literally 'opening up' a 'harnessed' opponent, in the manner of a crude can opener! The blade was secured by steel strips or 'languets' intended to reinforce the staff and frustrate the action of lopping off the head of the weapon.

Edmund Beaufort, 2nd Duke of Somerset, cornered at the 1st Battle of St Albans, fought valiantly before a blow from a poleaxe felled him.

The war hammer, a similarly unglamorous tool, was about 75cm long, a weapon which could be used from horseback or on foot. The handle, fashioned either in wood or steel, ended in a pick head with a stubby spike or hammer on the reverse. Richard III is credited with wielding a war hammer to deadly effect, in his last fight at Bosworth [1].

war hammer

The horseman's lance was still in use but it had grown much heavier than the original Norman spear from which it was derived. It was carried somewhat awkwardly, couched under the arm, and was used for thrusting. The weight was such that the weapon had to be held with the point angled across the saddle, a difficult business that could only be accomplished with diligent training. When used on foot, the shaft was generally cut down in length to make it easier to handle.

The medieval knight's sword had reached the apex of its development at this time, before being eclipsed in the next century by the *espada robera*, or rapier as we know it. The blade was designed for both cut and thrust and was long and

15th Century sword

elegantly tapered; it had a full grip that could be hefted in one or two hands. Its simple *quillons* (the cross bar guarding the hilt) were curved or straight, and a wheel, pear or kite shaped pommel completed the design.

This was the *hand and a half* or *bastard* sword, the very 'King of Swords'. Such precision instruments were reserved for the gentry and were extremely expensive to buy. The commoners carried a simpler, lighter and considerably cheaper sidearm: a short single-edged blade with quillons that curved around and up to the hilt to provide a form of crude knuckle-guard.

By this time the knightly shield had also disappeared from use, being impossible to operate with a *hand and a half* and also made redundant by the use of fine plate armours. Archers engaged in siege operations would utilise a thick wooden shield, like a small door, the *pavise*. A small round target or *buckler* was used with a sword to parry and punch. Thus the gallants of the day, strolling with their slung bucklers clanking against their sword hilts, became 'swashbucklers'.

Both Gentlemen and commons would carry a dagger: the long bladed *rondel*, with tapering triangular blade, hardwood grip, disc guard and pommel. The *ballock knife* was also used and featured a wooden handle with two rounded protuberances on the pommel creating a decidedly suggestive form!

ballock knife

Daggers were handy both as tool and as weapon: they might be used to stab an opponent or to plant vegetables, as the situation required. In battle the thin-bladed knife could be used to deliver the *coup de grace* to an armoured enemy, either thrust directly through the eye slit of a steel visor or into the armpit or genitals.

Knights, regardless of their prestige, mobility and quality of weaponry, only made up a small proportion of the 15th Century army. They were joined in battle by an array of archers, billmen, spearmen, bombardiers (who operated the cannon) and more. The type of weaponry utilised in battle often depended on the nationality of the men involved, each country having preferences for certain weapons. A Commander-in-Chief might recruit specialised mercenaries such as hand gunners.

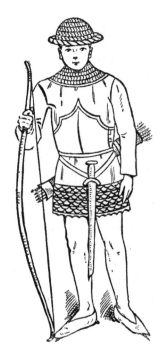

The longbow, simply termed the 'bow' or 'livery bow' until the 16th Century, was never deployed in significant numbers on the continent and therefore remained a peculiarly English weapon. Retained or liveried archers normally carried their own bows, but, in the long progress of the Hundred Years War (1337-1453), the Office of Ordnance began issuing standardised kit for archers on a campaign to replace those being lost or damaged. Quantities of bows were manufactured to a standard or government pattern, much like the infantry musket of following centuries.

Yew was the preferred timber for longbow manufacture, though ash, elm and wych-elm were also used. The weapon was usually between 5'7" (1.675m) and 6'2" (1.850m) in length, the cross section corresponded to a rounded 'D' with a draw weight of between 80-120lbs, (40-60 kilos). For comparison, a modern target bow has an average draw of around 45lbs!

Arrows were crafted from a variety of woods. Roger Ascham, tutor to Elizabeth I and a noted 16th Century authority, advocated aspen as the most suitable, although ash, alder, elder, birch, willow and hornbeam were also used. The shafts were generally around 2'6" (75cm) long, the fletching formed from grey goose feathers. Arrowheads came in a variety of forms: flat, hammer headed, barbed or wickedly sharp pointed piles or bodkins, designed to punch through plate and mail. 'Livery quality' arrows were issued to retainers, 'standard' grade were just that and 'sheaf' arrows came in bundles of two dozen [2].

At each extremity the bow was tipped with cowhorn, grooved to take the linen string. When not in use the stave was carried, unstrung, in a cloth

cover. To draw his bow, the archer gripped the stave with his left hand around its middle, where the circumference of the wood was around 4½" (12cm), holding the string with his right hand. He then forced the centre of the bow away from him to complete the draw, using the full weight of his body to assist, rather than relying on the strength of his arm alone. Such strength, stamina and expertise demanded constant drill and indeed practice at the village butts for the 'men of the grey goose feather' was enforced by statute. Such was the power needed that the archer needed to wear a leather or horn 'bracer' strapped to his wrist to protect him against the vicious snap of the bowstring, and the arrow thus shot could kill at two hundred yards.

Properly deployed, the bow had proved to be a devastating, battle-winning weapon; many who fought for Lancaster or York would already have seen active service in the French Wars. During the Wars of the Roses, English soldiers were continually on the receiving end of a hail of

Battle of Crecy, 26 August 1346
The English longbow triumphed over the crossbow.

arrows shot from the longbow, something they had not experienced in France. The use of the longbow raised the number of casualties considerably, as an arrow wound was agonizing as well as instantaneous, without the numbness caused by a high velocity bullet. It has been estimated that during the Palm Sunday Field of Towton in 1461, if each archer loosed four dozen arrows, then an astonishing one million shafts, with a gross weight of forty tons, fell across the field [3]. Gentlemen, secure in fine plate armour, enjoyed greater protection than did their predecessors, but the rank and file were less fortunate, relying on the cheaper flexible padded garments known as 'jacks'. At the Battle of Stoke in 1487 the Earl of Lincoln's ill-harnessed Irish kerns (or foot soldiers) were shot down in droves. Furthermore, improved armour did not render a knight invulnerable; when Lord Clifford unwisely removed his bevor (a protector for the neck and lower face over which the helmet was worn) to gulp down some water in the extended skirmish at Dintingdale, he was pierced by an arrow through the throat.

The other main projectile weapon used in the 15th Century was the crossbow, which was both a powerful and sophisticated weapon, so  much so that it required a rather complex arrangement of pulleys and cords, operated by windlass, to span (i.e. to draw the cord back to the locking position ready to shoot). The draw weight might be as great as 1,000lbs (500k), powerful enough to punch the stubby bolt through several files of unlucky foot soldiers. The very great and obvious disadvantage of using the crossbow was the slow rate of shooting and the cumbersome process of reloading.

The crossbowman tended to carry with him a *pavise* to afford cover while he spanned his bow, and he could shoot perhaps twice in a minute, whereas the longbowman could loose up to a dozen aimed flights in the same time – his arrows would be ready, 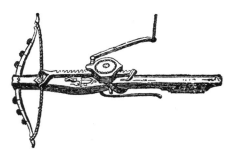 planted in the ground before him. Interestingly, this rapid fire equates to Tommy Atkins' rate of fire in 1914. Much favoured on the continent, the crossbow was little used in England.

For the lowly infantry man, a weapon still in use during the mid 15th Century was the 'bill' – a crude but highly effective hybrid of an agricultural tool and an implement of war. An 8' (2.4m) pole was adorned with a slicing blade (good for cutting hedgerows) along with a spike for stabbing and a hook for tripping an opponent.

English billmen, like their more celebrated contemporaries, the archers, fought in well-drilled companies. They wielded their weapons with a fearsome and deceptive ease that came of long practice.

By the later decades of the 15th Century, first Swiss halberds and later Swiss pikes made an appearance and soon became dominant; it was a Swiss pike that brought the quixotic career of Charles the Bold of Burgundy to its bloody end. However, Swiss pike tactics, invincible in the right circumstances, did not always work well in Britain, as James IV of Scotland found to his cost at Flodden in North Northumberland in 1513, when unsuitable ground caused the advance to fall into disarray and to lose vital cohesion.

The 15th Century also saw artillery become a dominant force in battle. A 'train' – the collective term for the artillery and the accompanying people and tools needed to work it – would comprise guns, gunners, gunners' mates (or matrosses), labourers, pioneers, carpenters, ammunition carts, mobile forges and a panoply of tools necessary to serve the iron monsters. Henry V put all this to good use during the French Wars when he bombarded the formidable walls of Le Mans in 1419. The walls gave out after only a few days [4]. 'Bombard' was a generic term, used to describe a large siege gun; in this era there was no standardisation of calibres [5]. In April 1464, as King Edward IV was preparing to march North, he caused his siege train to be made ready and this included: 'the great ordnance of England' – the 'Dijon', 'London', 'Newcastle', 'Edward' and 'Richard Bombartel' [6].

Monstrous guns like the ones named above had to be fired from ground level from behind hinged timber shutters, which were rather like a larger version of the archer's shield. Firing the guns was extremely hazardous even without the malevolent attentions of the enemy, as most guns were loaded at the breech. If fired without incident, the blast was accompanied by a vast discharge of sulphurous residue that cloaked the siege lines in a pall of greasy smoke. Transportation of the guns was an area of major difficulty: large teams of draught horses or oxen were required; 'pioneers' were part of the train and went ahead in order to level the roads over which the guns must pass, which were generally appalling.

Another weapon, growing in significance and potency, was the smaller handgun or 'gonne'. These were little more than miniature cannon, lashed to a basic wooden stock, called 'hagbutts'. The hagbutts were held under the arm or over the shoulder, rather than pressed into the shoulder as with a modern firearm. Once loaded with powder and shot, the gun was fired by means of a length of slow match, the burning end of which was applied to a touchhole, drilled into the side of the breech.

The late 15th Century also saw the creation of skilfully and beautifully made Italian armour. Its design aimed to maximise deflection and provide good defence in vulnerable areas such as the shoulders, elbows and knees. Ribs were fashioned on exposed parts of the body in order to deflect a

Suit of Gothic Armour

killing blow [7]. German armourers moved this concept onwards toward the 'Gothic' style, with an emphasis on uncompromising lines, swept by heavy fluting. A harness of this period might weigh around 60lbs (27.2 kilos), and would not greatly inhibit the mobility of a robust man trained since boyhood to move and fight in armour [8]. Indeed, medieval knights, even when fighting on foot, frequently bore a less onerous burden than the average 'Tommy' of World War One when he went 'over the top' burdened with rifle and pack, ammunition bandoliers, wire and tools.

The Italian and German styles came together in Flanders, a flourishing centre of manufacture where Italian armourers produced a hybrid style that featured the flexible, fluted plates of

Funerary momunent of Ralph Neville, 1st Earl of Westmorland
Staindrop Church, County Durham

the Gothic combined with the more rounded *pauldrons* [shoulder defences] and *tassets* [thigh guards] of their native style. Many of these pieces were sold in England, which is demonstrated by their regular appearance in funerary monuments.

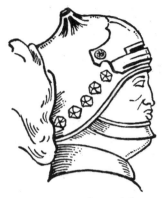

Bascinet of one of the Neville Family Brancepeth, Durham

For head protection, the stylish *sallet* form of helmet was popular from the mid 15th Century onwards; the rear of the elegantly curved brim was swept downward into a pointed tail to provide extra protection for the vulnerable areas at the back of the head and neck. Usually provided with a fixed or moveable visor, the sallet was accompanied by the *bevor*, which afforded protection to the throat and lower face. Although knights could move freely even in full plate, thirst and heat exhaustion were constant threats even in winter campaigning. Dressing for battle was best achieved at leisure, before the enemy was in the field, as a contemporary author, writing c.1450, explains:

To arme a man, firste ye must set on Sabatones *[armoured over-shoes]* and tye them up on the shoo with small points *[laces]* that woll not breke. And then griffus *[greaves, plate defences for the calves]* and then cuisses *[thigh defences]* and ye breche *[leggings]* of mayle. And the Tonlets. An the Brest and ye Vambras *[upper arm defences]* and ye rerebras *[lower arm]* and then gloovis *[plate gauntlets]*. And then hand his daggere up on his right side. And then his shorte sworde on his lyfte side in a round rynge all naked to pull it out lightli *[the sword is carried without a scabbard, hung in a ring for quick release]*. And then put his cote upon his back. And then his basinet *[Bascinet – a form of helmet in use prior to the sallet]* pyind up on two greet staples before the breste with a dowbill bokill *[double buckle]* behynde up on the back for to make the basinet sitte juste. And then his long swerd *[sword]* in his hande. And then his pensil in his hande peynted of St. George or of oure ladye to bless him with as he goeth towarde the felde and in the felde' [9].

While knights and men at arms would wear full harness, archers tended to favour padded *jacks* or *brigandines*, fabric garments that were finished with plates of steel or bone riveted between the inner and outer layers or, in the cheaper version, simply padded and stuffed with rags and tallow (animal fat). These 'jacks' were far cheaper, lighter and, for many purposes more practical – some were fitted with sleeves of mail to afford protection for the arms.

Though archers traditionally eschewed leg harness, billmen and men at arms would wear whatever they could afford or were able to loot, the seasoned campaigner augmenting his kit from the spoil of dead and captives. As an alternative to the more expensive sallet the foot might rely on the more basic 'kettle' hat, the forerunner in style to the 'tin hats' worn by Allied troops in both World Wars of the 20th Century.

Very few of the confrontations between Yorkists and Lancastrians involved siege warfare. Progress made in the science of gunnery had begun to make the traditional architecture of the medieval castle very vulnerable as the walls were too high and too narrow in section to withstand shot. An 'artillery fort' was a new development and entailed a bastion fitted with gun ports that allowed the inhabitants to defend themselves with gunfire. The trend moved away from building castles as part-fortress, part-residence towards a more specialised kind of fortification, with no domestic function. In Scotland, James III contemplated a chain of artillery forts along the banks of the Forth Estuary, although in practice only one of these, at Ravenscraig in Fife, was ever completed.

On a more domestic note, north of the border the increasing power of ordnance and handguns fuelled a variation on the standard form of Scottish tower; this was the 'Z' plan, where two slanted wings projected from the gables, fitted with gun loops to sweep along the long elevations, front and rear.

Even though artillery had diminished the status of castles as centres of resistance, guns remained expensive to procure and difficult to move. The various sieges of the Lancastrian-held strongholds in Northumberland 1461-1464, were conducted with an artillery train in attendance but only once were the great guns deployed in earnest. This was at Bamburgh Castle and the ordnance was brought into play with considerable reluctance. Bamburgh was a major bastion against the Scots and slighting such a key fortress was better avoided.

Bamburgh Castle - ordnance was brought into play with considerable reluctance

Perhaps the most prolonged and celebrated siege of the Wars of the Roses was the siege of Harlech, the core bastion of Lancastrian sentiment in

North Wales. This great, concentric fortress, a masterpiece of Edwardian design, occupies an elevated position which allowed re-victualling (stocking up of supplies) from the sea. Harlech resisted for the best part of seven years, holding out even when Jasper Tudor, the castellan, fled to Ireland. Jasper left Henry Tudor, the future Henry VII, in the care of the highly competent captain, Sir David ap Jevan ap Einion, and the garrison surrendered only on the most favourable of terms. Sieges were uncomfortable and expensive for the besieger, as well as being cramped, insanitary and dangerous for the besieged. If both sides could find an honourable way out, then this was a sensible outcome.

Field fortifications featured in a number of battles. When Richard Neville, Earl of Salisbury, was caught with inferior numbers at Blore Heath in 1459, he sought to consolidate what was already a strong defensive position by digging a ditch to cover the rear and erecting a wooden palisade to the front. Experienced men could construct these works in a very short time; in wooded landscape timber was in good supply and the army would have skilled pioneers in its ranks. The labour proved worthy of the effort, as suggested by the age old military maxim 'sweat saves blood': the Lancastrians failed to pierce the line.

Nearly a year later, in a miserable, sodden July, it was the Lancastrians, at Northampton, who placed their faith in a wet ditch and a timber palisade, studded with guns – this time to disastrous effect. Not only did unseasonable rainfall flood the gun pits and soak their powder, but the treacherous Lord Grey of Ruthin 'sold out' to Richard Neville, Earl of Warwick. Grey's men actually helped the Yorkist attackers to climb the palisade. Needless to say, the remainder of the Lancastrian line was taken in the flank and simply 'rolled up': 'rolling up the flank' occurs when a linear formation is struck from the side or flank, causing it to crumple.

In February 1461, Warwick himself placed great trust in elaborate entrenchments when preparing to meet Queen Margaret's host by St Albans, (later to be called the 2nd Battle of St Albans). A quantity of prepared positions were dug, augmented by a liberal sowing of caltraps – the anti-personnel and anti-equine devices of their day – with an array of spiked nets, hinged mantlets and other elaborate contrivances. Bad intelligence, slow thinking and possibly treachery confounded the complex scheme, which was foiled by a flank attack. Despite all this, the turncoat Sir Andrew Trollope was spiked nastily on a caltrap and was painfully unable to move. As he boasted at the time, this obliged his enemies to come to him, and he slew fifteen of them [10]! This demonstrates the danger of relying on a static defence: it transfers the initiative to the enemy, who decides when, where and how to attack.

During the Wars of the Roses there was a profound change in naval architecture, which witnessed a move away from the design of the cumbersome and ubiquitous 'round ship' of the early medieval period, toward the sleeker, Elizabethan *men o' war*. The medieval round ships were only twice as long as they were broad, fat bellied, slow to steer and with a fixed, square mainsail; they were jacks of all trades which for conversion into warships had timber decks, or 'castles' added, fore and aft. Tactics were restricted to grappling and boarding, missile power being provided by the archers on board. Even ramming was difficult, although the earlier 'cog', steered by an oar, had been superseded by the more sophisticated 'nef' fitted with a rudder mechanism [11].

At sea, as on land, guns made a significant difference. There are references from the early 1400s to ordnance on board ships but, initially, only light pieces were mounted in the two elevated castles, their function was to 'enfilade' (provide flanking fire) when men were attempting to board the enemy vessel, rather than aiming to sink the other ship entirely. In order to bear the weight of ordnance, the raised decks had to be strengthened and were augmented by several tiers rising and bristling with cannon. The guns were also positioned overlooking the internal elevations of the ship to further discourage unwelcome intruders.

The art of war, as practised during the Wars of the Roses, was directly influenced by the protracted struggle of the Hundred Years War which England fought with France between 1337 and 1453; many of the knights and common soldiers who fought as Lancastrians or Yorkists had seen action in France. The Wars of the Roses, however, were distinguishable by an enthusiasm for the shedding of noble blood that had rarely been seen in France. If captured alive during a medieval battle, a Knight was a great prize – a captive to be ransomed for the highest possible price. Private grudges and expediency however, demanded that the gentry who lost a fight during the Wars of the Roses could expect scant quarter and it was the common soldier who might receive greater clemency in defeat:

> 'King Edward told me that in all the battles which he had won, as soon as he had gained victory, he mounted his horse and shouted to his men that they must spare the common soldiers and kill the lords of which none or few escaped' [12].

The military system used during the Wars of the Roses originated in the reign of Edward III (1327-1377). In order to ensure a steady stream of capable soldiers who were available to fight in France, Edward opted to hire the services of his lords on a contract basis. Before this the King could only rely on his lords owing him forty days of 'knight service' after which they could decide whether to follow him into battle or not. This new system provided a reliable supply of trained fighting men and the monarch, as Commander-in-Chief, entered into formal engagements with experienced captains, providing indentured contracts in writing. Captains were bound to provide an agreed number of men, at established rates, for a given period. Frequently it was the magnates who acted as main contractors, sub-contracting knights, men at arms and archers in turn [13].

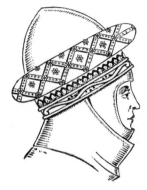

Bascinet and Orle
Sir Humphrey Stafford

By the mid 15th Century, this system created a reservoir of trained manpower – a ready supply of recruits at the disposal of the most powerful families. The contract system also meant that the lords were used to binding their retainers into military service via indentures and annuities. Humphrey Stafford, 1st Duke of Buckingham, who was killed at Northampton in 1460, had ten knights and twenty seven esquires in his service. One of these knights, Sir Edward Grey, was granted a life annuity of £40 in 1440. Men further down the social scale might receive annual emoluments of £10-£20 [14]. The King also had the power to issue what were termed 'Commissions of Array', which empowered his officers to call up local militias who, in theory at least, were to be the best armed and accoutred men from each village in the county. Although this system was time honoured it was much open to abuse; the antics of Falstaff in Shakespeare's *'King Henry IV Part 1'* provide a comic parody [15].

War has always been a hazardous enterprise. In the 15th Century a commander had limited forces at his disposal, and a single, significant defeat in the field would be likely to ruin his cause and not infrequently his person. Defeated generals fared badly in the Wars of the Roses: Somerset at St Albans, York at Wakefield, Northumberland at Towton, the younger Somerset at Hexham, his brother at Tewkesbury, Warwick at Barnet, Richard III at Bosworth and Lincoln at Stoke were all killed on the field or executed after the fight. Communications depended on the use of flags, and keeping the men fed and watered was a constant headache. The spectre of treachery was as omnipresent as Banquo's ghost.

In an attempt to avoid such a fate, a commander always attempted to deploy his men on favourable ground and to shun battle if the odds seemed unfavourable. In the dangerous game of cat and mouse that unfolded during the Tewkesbury campaign of 1471, Margaret of Anjou avoided contact several times, leaving the army of Edward IV looking faintly ridiculous, drawn up in battle array but without an enemy in sight!

The first step in preparing for battle was information-gathering. In a time of bad roads and slow communication, gathering intelligence about the movements of enemies and allies was a vital and difficult task. Misinformation could mean catastrophe – as Richard Duke of York discovered when he grossly underestimated the number of his foes and decided to commit to battle at Wakefield in 1460. He was killed in the fray. Once an informed decision to fight was made, a period of preparation followed. First a battle site and a campsite had to chosen. This took a great deal of logistical planning as armies consisted not only of fighting men but an array of cattle, flocks of sheep, goats, pigs and poultry in order to provide fresh meat, along with labourers, tradesmen, families, prostitutes, sutlers, farriers, barber-surgeons, quacks, vintners, fletchers, bowyers, smiths, armourers and carpenters. The army would also need a supply of small beer, which most people drank in preference to risking polluted water. The gentry would also need their comforts: wines, foodstuffs, pavilions and fine harness. Each great lord would march with his travelling household, and priorities over billeting could lead to dangerous squabbles (such as that which broke out between the Herberts and the Courtenays before the battle of Edgecote in 1469).

While the army was on the march, *hobilars* or light horsemen, sometimes called *prickers*, were deployed for scouting and vedette work (this was essentially patrolling and outpost duty). Using such intelligence and his own skill and experience in the field, a commander might then assess the potential battle ground, always seeking the position of best tactical advantage. Though the elements – harsh weather, mist and darkness – could combine to upset the best laid plans, late medieval captains were, for the most part, literate, and would have a theoretical as well as practical knowledge of tactical planning. Many would have read classical authors, such as the late Roman theorist, Vegetius, whose *Epitoma Rei Militaris* was revised in the 15ᵗʰ Century by Christine de Pisan. De Pisan also wrote *Livre des Fais D'Armes et de Chevalerie,* translated and popularised by Caxton as *The Book of the Fayttes of Armes and Chyvalrye.*

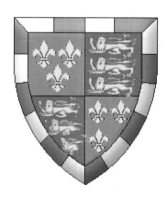

Heraldic Shield
Henry Beaufort
Duke of Somerset

Once a course of action was decided upon, the commanders of either side would manoeuvre their men in preparation for battle in full view of the enemy; each side thus knew when the time had come to engage. The armies were marshalled into three divisions or 'battles': the van or vaward, the main battle and the rear or rearward. Deployment was in linear formation, each company arranging itself under the banner of a captain or lord. Banners were important as morale boosters, signalling devices and rallying points. The use of liveries also promoted some degree of uniformity and consisted of a loose tunic or tabard worn over a jack or harness in the lord's colours. Unfortunately, this modest system of identification also produced moments of confusion such as during the Battle of Barnet in 1471, when in thick fog Lord Montagu's men mistook the Earl of Oxford's badge with its *star* and stream for King Edward's *sun* and stream, with disastrous consequences.

Before combat began, knights and men at arms dismounted in order to fight on foot. Horses were sent to the rear, to be mounted only when the enemy was in rout – pursuit of the beaten foe was rigorous and merciless.

A wealthy captive in the French Wars could be taken for ransom, but a lord whose lands stood to be attainted (taken from him along with his title) had no commercial value. Personal animosities were also a constant factor: when Edward IV rode triumphantly into York in1461 he would have seen the decapitated and rotting heads of his own father, brother and uncle staring down on him from Mickelgate Bar – a gatehouse on the city walls. The heads were of Richard Duke of York, Edmund Earl of Rutland and Richard Neville, Earl of Salisbury and had been fixed there after the earlier Lancastrian victory at Wakefield.

Most battles in the Wars of the Roses opened with an archery duel, regular volleys thudding home into tightly packed ranks, inflicting fatalities and serious wounds. In all probability, the archers, like the billmen, remained posted with their own companies rather than being formed into a separate

arm. Archers would advance a few paces from the line, shoot and then retake their places for the mêlée to follow. Due to the sheer effectiveness of this opening move, a contemporary chronicler observed: 'After the third or fourth, or at the very most the sixth draw of the bow, men knew which side would win' [16]. At the Battle of Towton in 1461, in bitter sleet, Thomas Neville, Lord Fauconberg, took advantage of poor visibility to move forward his Yorkist archers before they loosed the mass of shafts that flicked into the tightly packed Lancastrians. Having shot, his men then stepped smartly back whilst the archers of Henry Beaufort, 3rd Duke of Somerset, misgauging the range, shot into empty ground! Their own arrows were swiftly returned by their opponents and so galling was the Yorkist volley that the

Lancastrians had no recourse other than to advance to contact. Such was the power of the longbow under talented command.

These preliminaries probably lasted only a short time before the side which was suffering the most was compelled to advance. The movement would be ordered rather than swift, sergeants bellowing orders to keep the ranks dressed. Cohesion was all-important; the divisions that could maintain both order and momentum stood the best chance of breaking a more disordered foe. Although armies were deployed in linear formation, with opposing divisions aligned, this neat arrangement could go awry if the weather and the terrain conspired against them, as in the fog of Barnet mentioned above. A commander with a good eye for ground might try to deploy an ambush party for a flank attack; Somerset attempted this at Towton and Edward IV did the same at Tewkesbury ten years earlier. Tactical innovation, however, was hampered by poor communications on the field. The commander's inability to influence the outcome once battle was in full flow also placed a severe check on imaginative deployments or re-deployments.

Once battle was joined in earnest, the combat became an intensely personal affair, a hacking, stamping mêlée of bills and other polearms, sword and axe. Men, half blind in their armour, were soon beleaguered by raging thirst and would swiftly reach exhaustion and become disorientated; dust and the steam from thousands of sweating men would further obscure any wider view. Few knights would be killed by a single blow; rather, a disabling wound would bring the sufferer to his knees, exposing him to a further flurry of blows. More often than not, his skull would then be shattered and he would be pierced through the visor or groin by daggers, hacked by bills, stamped on, kicked and slashed. It was not a swift death, nor an easy one. Illustrations from the period show the field heaped with

The mêlée

the press of the slain, garnished by a slew of severed limbs. Blood would run in rivulets, splattering the living who would resemble a species of berserk butcher, their livery and harness becoming clotted with tissue and gore.

Once one side broke, leading to a rout, casualties would begin to mount. Armoured men trying to flee towards horses tethered at a distance would be easy prey. Those less encumbered, or not enfeebled with wounds, might survive the race, but many would not. The victors, their horses brought forward by their grooms, would be swooping and circling like hawks. Abbot Whethamstede, who may have been an eyewitness at the 2nd Battle of St Albans in 1461, wrote of the Earl of Warwick's men:

> The southern men, who were fiercer at the beginning, were broken quickly afterwards, and the more quickly because looking back, they saw no one coming up from the main body of the King's army, or preparing to bring them help, whereupon they turned their backs on the northern men and fled. And the northern men seeing this pursued them very swiftly on horseback; and catching a good many of them, ran them through with their lances [17].

A mass grave, excavated in the last decade on the field of Towton, has provided a grim insight into the sheer nastiness of 15th Century warfare: thirty seven skeletons were unearthed, most of which had suffered a series of horrific head injuries: puncture wounds and calamitous fractures. There is evidence of specific and deliberate dagger thrusts to the back of the skull, almost surgical in precision – either the coup de grâce or cold blooded execution. In either event, the victim would have been stripped of head protection at the fatal moment [18].

By contemporary standards the medical services available were both rudimentary and sparse. The perceived presence of 'imbalanced humours' were the reason for carrying out bleedings: the deliberating cutting and releasing of blood in order to restore balance and allow the body to rejuvenate. Quacks would cast horoscopes and would peddle bizarre potions, and wounds were painfully but sensibly cauterised with hot pitch. Interestingly, herbal anaesthetics were by no means unknown, and surgical techniques were perhaps more sophisticated than might be assumed. One of the dead exhumed from the Towton grave pit showed evidence of a previous injury, a massive facial trauma, probably caused by the swing of a blade. Investigations have shown that this terrible wound had been treated and that the shattered bone and tissue had been repaired; our man would not have been beautiful, but he had survived. Although armies did not field a medical corps *per se*, each contingent would have surgeons, contracted by indenture. Sieges, where terms for surrender had been negotiated, were habitually concluded with arrangements for the care and transport of the wounded.

As discussed, most fatal injuries were caused by blows to the head, as the mute remains from excavated grave pits disclose. The bodies of the English dead from Otterburn [1388], whose remains were discovered beneath the nave of Elsdon Church during repairs in the 19th Century, bear this out. Slashing and stabbing wounds, though ghastly, were not always fatal; secondary complications such as septicaemia and peritonitis invariably were. Gerhard von Wesel, travelling in England in 1471, has left an eyewitness account of the army of King Edward IV as the survivors of Barnet trudged wearily back into London, remarking that 'many of their followers were wounded, mostly in the face or the lower part of the body, a very pitiable sight' [19]. These, it must be remembered, were the victors.

Campaigns of the period tended to be highly mobile and of relatively short duration. As mentioned above, adequate logistical provision for keeping large bodies in the field was a particular problem, as was the need to find cash to pay wages. In common with other periods, more men died from disease and want than they did from enemy action. Dysentery was a major killer, as were cholera and typhus. Plague also stalked the armies; the late medieval era has been described as 'the golden age of bacteria' [20] with perhaps thirty or more outbreaks occurring between the first onslaught (in 1348) and 1487. French mercenaries in the service of

Henry Tudor were blamed for introducing the 'sweating sickness' (or 'flu' as we might call it) that killed off two mayors of London and six aldermen in barely a week, in 1485 [21].

With the main slaughter ended, the field would be covered with many wounded, too weakened to drag themselves from the press. Some would be rescued or tended by their women, who lined the edges of the field like a crowd at a Saturday afternoon football match. These women fulfilled a vital and dangerous role as water carriers and 'paramedics' during battle, and at least one battlefield, Harlaw in Scotland, is said to contain the grave pit of the female dead. The wounded on the losing side may have been speedily dispatched or simply stripped and left bloodied, prey for the flocks of scavengers who would steal over the stricken field as the light faded – human jackals.

Time and romance have, over the intervening years, cast a veil of pageantry over the harsh realities of medieval combat. The truth is somewhat less attractive. Although they lacked the scale and widespread devastation of modern wars and were devoid of the full horror of industrialised conflict, warfare in the 15th Century was every bit as terrible.

Notes:

[1] Norman A V P and Pottinger D, *'English Weapons and Warfare 499-1600 AD'* London 1966 p.137

[2] Bartlett C, *'The English Longbowman 1330-1515'* London 1985 pp.23-30

[3] Boardman A, *'The Battle of Towton'* England 1994 p.167

[4] Norman and Pottinger op. cit. p.137

[5] A survivor from this period and still to be viewed in Edinburgh Castle is 'Mons Meg' which may be considered typical of the heavy guns of this period. Cast in Flanders, around 1460, the barrel length is 13'2" (3.95m) with a bore of 19½" (49cm) – it fired a massive stone ball for a distance of up to two miles, see Norman and Pottinger op. cit. p.140. An even larger piece was cast by the renegade Hungarian smith Urban for the Ottoman Mehmet II. Urban had previously offered his services to the Byzantine Emperor, Constantine, who declined on the grounds of cost. The Sultan's purse was deeper and bought him a massive gun, cast in January 1453, which measured 26'8" and could shoot a 12cwt ball over a mile. The Emperor would soon have had cause to rue his parsimony as the piece was soon deployed against Constantinople's fabled walls, see Runciman, Sir Stephen, 'The Fall of Constantinople' England 1965 p.77-78.

[6] 'Edward' is featured in an inventory of 1475; the Master of Ordnance, John Sturgeon, handed into store at Calais '… divers parcels of the King's Ordnance and artillery, including a bumbardell [bombard] called 'The Edward'', see Blackmore H L, 'The Armouries of the Tower of London – Ordnance' HMSO 1976 p.33, also Haigh p.83, see [10] below.

[7] Blair C, 'European Armour' London 1958 p.77

[8] Norman and Pottinger op. cit. p.114

[9] Oakeshott R and Ewart A, 'Knight and his Weapons' London 1964 p.51

[10] Haigh P A, 'The Military Campaigns of the Wars of the Roses' London 1995 p.49

[11] Archibald E H H, 'The Wooden Fighting Ship' London 1968 p.6

[12] Philip de Commynes, 'The Memoirs for the Reign of Louis XI, 1461-1463' transl. Jones M 1972, p.187

[13] Wise T, 'The Wars of the Roses' London 1983 p.22 An esquire was a knight's attendant, a rank below in the feudal hierarchy. A squire was an aspiring knight, who had not yet been dubbed, from the French ecuyer the bearer of the knightly shield or ecu.

[14] Haigh op. cit. p.23

[15] In Act IV sc. i [Falstaff] 'If I be not ashamed of my soldiers I am a soused gurnet I have misused the King's press damnably.'

[16] Boardman op. cit. p.167

[17] Riley H T (ed.), *'Registrum Abbatis Johannis Whethamstede'* 1872, vol 1 pp.388-392

[18] Boardman op. cit. pp.181-183

[19] Bartlett op. cit. p.51

[20] Thrupp S L, *'The Problem of Replacement Rates in Late Medieval English Population'* ECHR 2nd Series 18 1965-1966

[21] Ibid p.18

PART FOUR

ORIGINS: THE FRENCH WARS AND THE

HOUSE OF LANCASTER

The leading magnates of the 15th Century were often related by complex threads of blood or marriage, many of them having some sort of family connection to the royal line. Throughout the medieval period, usurpation occured (the removal of a king because of his unacceptably bad rule), although it was contrary to God's law. Just such an event occurred in 1399 when the 'House of Lancaster' in the person of Henry Bolingbroke, the son of John of Gaunt, Duke of Lancaster, took the crown from his cousin, Richard II. Both men were grandsons of the late King Edward III.

Edward III fathered five sons and was the instigator of the French Wars also known as the 'Hundred Years War'. There was no higher aspiration for a gentleman than to excel in the arts of war, and Edward's expansionist policy into France promised wealth and glory for his lords as well as giving them a channel for their martial energies. The war began tentatively in 1337 when Edward attempted to secure continental allies using an expensive blend of bribes and diplomacy. When civil war broke out in the Duchy of Brittany, Edward saw it as an opportunity to become more deeply involved in the affairs of France.

Edward was not slow to exploit his chance and a series of minor but successful engagements were fought, such as those of Morlaix (1342) and

Mauron (1352). In 1346 a major trial of arms took place at Crécy, where the English won a stunning victory. Other triumphs followed: at Auberoche, at La Roche Derrien and finally at Poitiers in 1356. In this battle an English chevauchée led by the King's son Edward (who had the sobriquet 'the Black Prince', perhaps due to his blackened armour), was brought to bay by superior French forces,

Battle of Crécy, 26 August 1346

commanded by their King. Despite these odds, the English emerged victorious and the captured King of France was taken to join the King of Scots who was already imprisoned in the Tower [1].

The Treaty of Brétigny in 1360 brokered a peace which seemed to secure the gains the English had made, but hostilities were resumed in 1369. The Black Prince, by then a sick man, had won a final dazzling victory in Spain at Nájera three years earlier, but the tide had begun to turn. The last years of

Edward, the Black Prince

ORIGINS: THE FRENCH WARS AND
THE HOUSE OF LANCASTER

Edward III's reign lacked the brilliance of earlier times; the Black Prince finally died in 1376, succumbing to a 'malaise', a year before his father.

Prince Edward left a son, Richard, who with the death of his father and then his grandfather was crowned King of England in 1377 – he was just ten years old. Clearly, a regent was needed to rule England until he was of a suitable age to govern; the obvious candidate was one of his father's younger brothers, his powerful uncle John of Gaunt, the Duke of Lancaster, third son of Edward III.

By the time Richard II was old enough to take the reigns of power he had built up a personal clique, narrow in scope and generally unpopular. His sexuality was questionable, and opposition soon grew toward his chosen friends – opposition led by the Duke of Gloucester, with the Earls of Arundel and Warwick. When John of Gaunt departed to pursue his own dynastic ambitions in Spain [2] Richard found himself embarrassed when, lobbying Parliament for the additional taxation needed to prop up England's deteriorating position in France, the members first insisted on the removal of his coterie from court. By nature autocratic, Richard refused and Parliament retaliated by impeaching his Chancellor, the Earl of Suffolk.

Richard deemed such conduct tantamount to treason, especially when Parliament insisted on establishing a commission to oversee the King's affairs – an intolerable impertinence. But Parliament was not to be deflected, and in 1388 a number of the king's favourites were outlawed and some were even executed. The king appeared isolated and impotent; a committee of five 'Lords Appellant' became, in effect, a regency council. Not until May 1389 did Richard recover his nerve and his independence.

Towards the end of 1389 Gaunt returned from Spain and assumed the mantle of Elder Statesman, fostering some superficial harmony between the fractious king and the Lords Appellant. However, Richard was learning the art of duplicity and was cannily rebuilding his power-base around a fresh faction. After a peaceable interval of eight years he struck, arresting Warwick, Arundel and Gloucester – the men who had

John of Gaunt

objected to his personal friends. Although the first of these was simply exiled, the other two lost their lives. At the same time Parliament's wings were clipped – the King's star appeared at last to be in the ascendant. A quarrel between the two surviving Lords Appellant – Thomas Mowbray, Duke of Norfolk and Gaunt's son and heir Henry Bolingbroke – prompted the king to banish both of them.

On the death of John of Gaunt in February 1399, Richard recklessly seized an opportunity to restore his overstretched finances by confiscating John of Gaunt's vast estate, disinheriting young Bolingbroke and extending his banishment to a life term. Such open brigandry struck at the very souls of the magnates. If the King could pillage his nobles' coffers in this way, on a random pretext, no-one was safe. Richard's greed and desperation had led him to the edge of the abyss; he proceeded to leave himself completely exposed by embarking on an ill-conceived Irish expedition.

Henry Bolingbroke, not the calibre of man to stand by whilst his rightful inheritance was stolen from him, launched a successful coup. Magnates and commons swelled to his banner and the King, returning across the Irish Sea in August, found himself isolated and powerless. Within a month, after the intervention of Henry Percy, 1st Earl of Northumberland, Richard had surrendered and given up his throne to Henry Bolingbroke who was crowned King Henry IV. Richard was imprisoned in Pontefract Castle, where he died: inevitably, foul play was suspected. The House of Lancaster had arrived:

> *'Heaven knows, my son,*
> *By what by-paths, and indirect crook'd ways.*
> *I met this crown; and I myself know well.*
> *How troublesome it sat upon my head.'*

Shakespeare, Henry IV Part 1

The many difficulties of Richard's reign had been compounded by the financial pressure of the continuing French War. The epic resonance of the great victories of his grandfather's day had faded into a grim catalogue of attrition as the French, ably led by commanders such as Bertrand du Guesclin, steadily clawed back many of the English gains.

With all the uncertainties facing a usurper, his treasury empty and beset by these disturbances, Henry IV was in no position actively to renew hostilities in France. The gauntlet of the great trial with France was left to his son, Henry V, who succeeded to the throne on his father's death in 1413. Henry, Shakespeare's Prince Hal, was destined to become the very epitome of chivalry.

According to contemporary accounts Henry V was already impressive at twenty-five: tall, well built and handsome. He had a florid, clean-shaven face with a high forehead, a long and commanding nose, full red lips, hazel eyes and auburn hair cut in a pudding basin crop – the fashionable military

Henry V

haircut of the day. This may well be how he looked before ceaseless campaigning aged him prematurely and before he grew his beard. The contemporary sources also agree that he was unusually fit and muscular, wearing his armour 'like a light cloak' and, allegedly, being able to run down a deer. However, according to the French astrologer Jean Fusoris, who was presented to him in the summer of 1415, he looked more like a prelate than he did a soldier, despite his lordly manner and noble bearing.

Complex if dynamic and vital, reserved and secretive, icily cold, with complete self control, he was very difficult to know and to understand. He said little and listened much. He both wrote and spoke Latin as well as French and English, and had probably acquired some knowledge of Welsh. He possessed a large library to which he was always adding, and 'the most one can say with confidence about him is that friends and foes admired and feared him, and that they did not love him. The sole qualities with which the chroniclers credit him are military skill, strict and indeed harsh justice, and ostentatious piety.' [3]

Henry had won his spurs in the mêlée at Shrewsbury in 1403, when the Percy Earls of Northumberland rebelled against King Henry IV and the young Henry Percy was wounded in the face [4]. He had gone on to learn his trade in the course of suppressing the Welsh revolt of Owen Glendower. He revived the French Wars in earnest and his campaign to capture Harfleur in Normandy during the summer of 1415 ('Once more unto the breach, dear friends, once more; or close the wall up with our English dead!'), culminated in the greatest and best known of English victories: the Field of Agincourt, 25 October 1415.

Despite the scale of the catastrophe which had befallen them, the French were not cowed into immediate submission by the disaster; indeed they rallied with surprising resilience and even this, the greatest of England's many great victories, did not secure her war aims. Harfleur was quickly turned into an English frontier outpost, or *bastide*. In the following year the Earl of Dorset fought another brisk action at Valmont, devastating a far superior force under Bernard of Armagnac. Although there were some attempts at papal mediation, Henry V invaded France once again in the summer of 1417. He invaded the ancient city of Caen, seat of William the Conqueror and a formidable nut to crack, which had previously fallen to Edward III. Caen was bombarded and finally stormed; by the close of the campaigning season Henry controlled the whole of lower Normandy.

In the following spring the King prepared to attempt the seizure of Rouen, a prize that would unlock the entire duchy of Normandy. By this time the French had tired of Bernard of Armagnac, whom they killed. They then entrusted their war effort to John the Fearless, Duke of Burgundy. The Duke assumed joint control with the Queen (Isabella) of France, her husband King Charles VI being unfit to rule due to chronic mental illness.

The Duke of Burgundy did little to help the desperate citizens of beleaguered Rouen, who were finding out what an utterly ruthless opponent was Henry V of England [5]. By the middle of January 1419, the city was his. In the late summer of that year an equally momentous event occurred: John the Fearless was murdered by a faction loyal to the recently deceased Bernard of Armagnac, whose place he had taken. This lunatic act of political folly had the effect of pushing the vengeful Burgundians into the arms of the English. The new Duke, Philip 'The Good', inherited a vast domain, secure in great wealth and connection. Phillip was a true politician; cautious, scheming and forever manoeuvring to his best advantage, he ruled his duchy for half a century.

John, Duke of Bedford

By December 1419, Philip Duke of Burgundy had concluded an alliance with Henry V, an accord sealed by the marriage of the King's brother, John, Duke of Bedford, to Philip's sister, Anne. In the following May, Henry began serious negotiations towards a permanent settlement with Queen Isabella and her poor, mad husband Charles VI. Henry had already agreed a power-sharing pact with Philip of Burgundy, whereby in effect the latter would, on the unification of the crowns of England and France, become Viceroy. Under the terms of the Treaty of Troyes in 1420, the Dauphin (the title for the son and heir of the French King) was brushed aside. The succession settled on the King of England; Henry would wed Princess Catherine, daughter of Charles and Isabella, and become Regent of France, holding the whole of Normandy and parts of Aquitaine in his own right.

Such a successful outcome did not bring an end to the campaigning, which continued against those forces still loyal to the slighted Dauphin Charles, who were neither impotent nor cowed. Henry was successful in capturing, after sieges, Montereau and Melum before he returned to England in triumph. In his absence from France, operations were entrusted to his volatile brother the Duke of Clarence, whose recklessness led to disaster at Beauge at Easter 1421: a French army, invigorated by a strong Scots contingent under the Earl of Buchan [6], destroyed him and most of his meagre forces.

Henry, true to form, reacted to the news of his brother's defeat and death with decisive calm; despite reduced numbers, the Earl of Salisbury was able to see off the Franco-Scots when they menaced the frontiers of Normandy. Late in the spring, the King again took to the field. As ever, the charisma of his name induced a particular paralysis amongst his enemies; by October he was standing beneath the walls of Meaux, recognising that the line of the Loire was the new battleground. In December 1421 his French wife produced an heir – the future King Henry VI.

Henry V won notable victories in France, and the terms of the Treaty of Troyes opened dazzling prospects. However, notwithstanding his success, at the close of 1421 Henry had no illusions about the stability of his gains. Everything depended on the continuation of two basic elements: the perceived magic of Henry's name and the durability of the Burgundian alliance. When Henry, the hero-king, succumbed to dysentery on 31 August 1422, the mainstay of the English effort was kicked away, leaving the Dauphin Charles undefeated and still in the field. France remained largely unconquered, and the occupied territories had to be held down by garrisons. *Occupation*, holding down enemy territory by force of arms, can never graduate to *conquest* until hearts and minds have been won and the population has come to identify with the invader. This assimilation was never achieved. The rapacity of the English naturally caused lasting resentment; in the long term, rule by jackboot is never successful.

Thus King Henry VI of England was to come into an inheritance of two kingdoms: one was a reality, the other largely titular for as long as the spurned Dauphin Charles could keep forces in the field. As Henry V prepared for death, pragmatic as ever, he gave instructions as to who should run these two kingdoms until his infant son came of age. In France the choice was obvious: his reliable brother John, Duke of Bedford, a mature and capable figure whose marriage to Philip's sister had cemented the Burgundian alliance. In England, matters were more complex. Henry's youngest surviving brother, Humphrey, Duke of Gloucester, was gifted and creative but he lacked the skills necessary for sustained diplomacy. Gloucester was to be Protector in England, but only for such periods as Bedford was detained in France.

A new force had recently entered the English polity – the Beaufort family, legitimised offspring of John of Gaunt's long term romantic liaison with his mistress Katherine Swynford, whose sister was married to Geoffrey Chaucer. Richard II had provided ample opportunity for the advancement of this ambitious brood, even if they were specifically excluded from any pretensions to the throne itself. Ablest of all was Henry Beaufort, Bishop of Winchester, by 1422 Chancellor of England and destined five years later to attain a cardinal's hat. He and Humphrey of Gloucester were already antipathetic. While he was guardian of the infant ruler, Henry Beaufort appointed yet another Beaufort as Duke of Exeter and a third brother was made Earl of Dorset, (later Duke of Somerset).

Throughout the whole of the medieval period, regency councils were notoriously prone to factionalism, and from the very outset the Beaufort family had a very loud voice indeed. By 1429 when the young king was formally crowned in Westminster Abbey, Bishop Beaufort had become Cardinal Beaufort and his relations with Gloucester had deteriorated even further. The adherents of both sides had attended the Leicester Parliament of three years earlier bearing cudgels, with the result that the assembly was dubbed 'The Parliament of Bats'.

While the Regency Council bickered in England, John, Duke of Bedford was attempting to maintain his nephew's cause in France. Henry's death might seriously have undermined the motive for the war and the direction in which it was going, but the English position showed no immediate signs of deterioration. Cardinal Beaufort had grown exceedingly rich from his emoluments as Chancellor of the Duchy of Lancaster and fees from numerous ecclesiastical lands. Gloucester, though a royal duke, held only modest estate and whilst Beaufort was happy to toe the official line of continued enmity with France, Humphrey had a great dislike for Philip of Burgundy.

The Dauphin Charles became Charles VII of France on the death of his father in October 1421, although his official coronation was delayed because of the English aggression (he was not finally crowned until Jeanne d'Arc had raised the siege of Orléans and made Rheims safe for the ceremony, until which time he retained the title of Dauphin). He could not manage to raise a sufficient force or find generals effectively to challenge the English in open field. Most importantly, the vital alliance between Burgundy and England held. Bedford, a highly competent commander in his own right, was endowed with the levels of patient diplomacy needed to deal with his slippery brother in law Philip of Burgundy, who controlled Paris and the north. As regent he also maintained the potentially fragile English hegemony in Normandy and Aquitaine.

'I'll hale the Dauphin headlong from his throne, -
His crown shall be the ransom of my friend;
Four of their lords I'll change for one of ours.
Farewell, my masters; to my task will I;
Bonfires in France forthwith I am to make,
To keep our great Saint George's feast withal;
Ten thousand soldiers with me I will take,
Whose bloody deeds shall make all Europe quake.'

Henry VI Part One: Act 1, Sc. i

Though not a warlike King, Charles VII of France was steadfast; he refused to be cowed completely by his formidable enemies. His shrunken court at Bourges acted as magnet for all men – and there were many – who chafed at being under the thumb of the sneering English or the perfidious Burgundians.

In April 1423, Bedford entered into a tripartite accord with Philip the Good of Burgundy and Jean V of Brittany. England held to this commitment when the Burgundians were faced with a Franco-Scottish force at Cravant in July 1423, where a combined Burgundian and English effort crushed the opposition. Despite the severity of this setback, Charles dispatched a grander expedition into Normandy the following summer. Again, the Scots were heavily involved; this time led by the Earl of Douglas. Bedford was joined by the Earl of Salisbury and they met the Dauphin's army at Verneuil in 1424. After a hard fought fight in great heat, where a wing of the English army was discomfited and broke away, Bedford won a victory for the English. Douglas was left dead on the field of battle with a score of French and Scottish lords.

It seemed beyond doubt that the English could still fight and win battles but Bedford's campaigns were no longer winning new territory – they were merely protecting what England already held. The principal beneficiary of these triumphs was Philip of Burgundy, whose lands had expanded to cover a quarter of France, and whose coffers were overflowing. By now the war was becoming a major drain on English resources and there were insufficient new gains to satisfy land-hungry knights. Furthermore, Philip – at the same time as receiving cash subsidies from Bedford – had begun to enter into clandestine talks with Charles VII. However much King Charles might have detested having dealings with a turncoat, he perceived that his only salvation lay in wrecking the Anglo-Burgundian alliance, thus dividing his foes.

In 1427, Brittany, possibly sensing which way the wind was blowing, broke from the tripartite accord of 1423 and threatened an attack on Normandy – held by the English. In an invigorated campaign, Bedford swiftly cowed Jean V of Brittany when the Earl of Suffolk rampaged, unchecked, through his lands. The Earl of Salisbury took Le Mans and in the summer of 1428 entered Paris. The English tide had reached its high water mark.

The English made for Orléans and by the start of October 1428 they stood before its walls. The siege began well but the Earl of Salisbury, an able commander, was mortally wounded by a stray roundshot. The Earl of Suffolk assumed command but was considerably less dynamic, and fresh defensive troops were able to enter the city. The English regained their aggressive posture, however, when Bull Talbot, the 'English Achilles', was appointed Earl of Shrewsbury, his career blossoming as he replaced Salisbury (on his death) as the driving force. The siege dragged on through the dismal heart of winter, and on 12 February 1429 the English Captain Fastolff defeated a French force under the Count of Clermont [7]. This

Battle of the Herrings, 12 February 1429

English victory was followed in March by the arrival of Jeanne the Maid, otherwise known as Jeanne d'Arc. This remarkable young woman's energy galvanized the defenders, who broke the siege with a series of daring attacks on the ring of English forts. Worse, Shrewsbury's withdrawal culminated in a disastrous rout at Patay, where both he and Fastolff were taken. Though her future successes were modest and Jeanne's career in arms ended in capture and incarceration followed by her infamous brutal death at the stake, the myth of the invincible English had been shattered. Jeanne's achievements seemed to sway Philip of Burgundy to ponder further about changing sides. Paris was threatened, and the Duke sought some pretext to switch his allegiance. He chose, cynically, to take offence when Bedford, now a widower, re-married: as mentioned above, Bedford's first wife Ann had been Philip's sister, a dynastic marriage made

Jeanne d' Arc

to cement the allegiance. For Philip of Burgundy her death allowed a welcome excuse to distance himself from the alliance. He also discovered a handy loophole in the Treaty of Troyes by construing the terms in a manner which allowed him to repudiate his allegiance to the English cause. Philip now produced a near masterstroke by proposing that a peace conference be convened with him acting as arbiter. Bedford's position was weakened by continued splits in the Council; the Beauforts by now had a pessimistic view of the war and were edging towards support for peace. Humphrey, Duke of Gloucester, wanted to maintain the fight.

The great Congress of Arras opened in July 1435. John, Duke of Bedford, already a very sick man, died in September and it was Cardinal Beaufort who led the English delegation. Bedford was scarcely laid to rest when Philip of Burgundy agreed terms with Charles VII, abandoning his former allegiance with England. This was treachery such that even the saintly Henry VI, then aged thirteen, could not forgive.

In 1436 the French recovered Paris while Philip of Burgundy hastened to demonstrate his new found commitment to the King by making an attempt on Calais, held by the English. Humphrey, Duke of Gloucester, in charge of the defence of Calais, soon saw him off and went on to harry Burgundian lands. Richard, Duke of York (grandson of Edward III's fourth son, Edmund Duke of York) was appointed as Bedford's successor in France. Richard took Dieppe before being replaced by the Earl of Warwick, assisted by Bull Talbot. They jointly took the field with Sir Thomas Kyriel and maintained the offensive.

At this time of mounting crisis England had a boy king, a divided Council and a resentful Parliament whose willingness to continue levying taxes was waning. Cardinal Beaufort and others of his faction were in favour of a pragmatic approach – peace with honour. It was obvious to this 'peace' faction that England was no longer capable of adding anything to her French territories; it was a just a matter of clinging to such land and power as could be salvaged. Henry VI had actually been crowned King of France in the Cathedral of Notre Dame in Paris on 2 December 1431 but the gesture was something of a sham: the true King of France was always crowned at Rheims, where he was anointed with St Remy's Holy Oil.

Charles VII of France

Humphrey of Gloucester, as champion of the 'war' faction, fired by the memory of the great days of Agincourt and Verneuil, was wedded to the romantic notion of continuing the struggle. Beaufort, however, favoured a dynastic marriage alliance to ensure a ceasefire, proposing a match between Henry VI and a princess of the Valois family, the royal family of France. This idea was rejected at the peace Congress of Arras. Gloucester on the other hand suggested a marriage between Henry and the daughter of Jean, Count of Armagnac, a union which would support the English position in Aquitaine and send a defiant message to the French. This was not to be. By 1442, Charles VII had assembled enough military might to cow Count Jean, who broke off negotiations. The English forces now engaged in propping up the remains of their empire in France.

Disobligingly, the French now failed to launch unimaginative and doomed mass frontal assaults of the kind which had characterised earlier battles. Under a new generation of professional captains, men like Dunois, La Hire and Xaintrailles, the French could now field a force of trained, professional foot soldiers, many of whom were ex-mercenaries, backed by a formidable train.

With Paris back in French hands, English outposts were cleared from the Ile de France, and the country north of the Seine. Charles VII, though not a great soldier, was certainly a ruthlessly efficient politician and a sound administrator; Philip the Good of Burgundy was gradually marginalised and his influence began to wane. A further peace convention was convened at Gravelines in 1439, but the negotiations swiftly foundered; Cardinal Beaufort would not consider making any terms more attractive than he'd offered four years earlier at Arras.

Despite their apparent intransigence, young King Henry supported the peace faction led by Cardinal Beaufort, Somerset and Suffolk who favoured a diplomatic solution to the French war. The drain on the treasury was enormous and the annual cost of war far exceeded royal revenues; the Duke of Gloucester's blustering was sounding increasingly hollow.

The peace faction moved swiftly to emasculate their rivals. The Duke of York (who supported Gloucester in maintaining the war) was sent into virtual exile to Ireland, whilst Gloucester was attacked obliquely when his wife was accused of being a witch. This was all trumped up nonsense of course, but it was credible nonsense: the duchess was convicted, publicly humiliated and imprisoned. Her husband, who was apparently without any power to protect her, was driven from public life because of the attendant scandal.

In France, Charles continued to whittle away the English outposts and maintained the pressure, sparring with Somerset in Aquitaine until both sides were exhausted. A new peace initiative was launched and discussions began at Tours in the spring of 1444. Suffolk acted as the principal English negotiator and the Truce of Tours was finally sealed in 1446. The truce confirmed that the English were in possession of the lands they still held, with a tacit admission that the rest was lost. By way of a dynastic marriage, the best that the young King of England could achieve was the hand of the sixteen year old Margaret of Anjou, daughter of Duke René of Bar and Lorraine. Duke René was the titular but impecunious King of Sicily, who was unable even to fund a dowry for his daughter. This young and spirited Princess arrived in England during April 1445. Although the fleet was magnificent, her sea passage was turbulent and she required several days of rest at Portsmouth. She had yet to meet her new husband; although they had officially married a month beforehand at Nancy, Suffolk had acted as proxy for the absent groom. Raffaeolo de Negra, an Italian correspondent, recalled a story current at the time:

> 'When the Queen landed in England the king dressed himself as a squire, and took her a letter which he said the king of England had written. While the queen read the letter the king took stock of her, saying that a woman may be closely observed while she is reading, and the queen never found out that it was the king

because she was so engrossed in the letter that she never looked at the king in his squire's dress' [8].

As John Gillingham points out, this was probably the *only* time that the twenty three year old Henry VI would enjoy an advantage over his strong-willed young wife. Had the king possessed the ability to glimpse the future, he might well have been tempted to ride in the opposite direction.

King Henry VI assumed his full responsibilities as monarch at a time when the need for strong kingship was needed. The qualities required for this role could be likened to those possessed by his father Henry V, a ruthlessly successful and unvanquished field commander who took real pleasure in the rigours and ferocity of combat: 'War without fire', he is said to have stated, 'is like sausages without mustard' [9].

By contrast, if we accept fully what his chaplain John Blackman asserts, Henry VI was extremely pious and morally incorruptible, as well as being unusually chaste:

'He was, like a second Job, a man simple and upright, altogether fearing the Lord God, and departing from evil. He was a simple man, without any crook of craft or untruth, as is plain to all. With none did he deal craftily, nor ever would say an untrue word to any, but framed his speech always to speak truth. This King Henry was chaste and pure from the beginning of his days. He eschewed all licentiousness in word or deed while he was young; until he was of marriageable age, when he espoused the most noble lady, Lady Margaret, daughter of the King of Sicily, by who he begat only one son, the most noble and virtuous prince Edward; and with her and toward her he kept his marriage vow wholly and sincerely, even in the absences of the lady, which were sometimes very long; never dealing unchastely with any other woman. Neither when they lived together did he use his wife unseemly, but with all honesty and gravity ...' [10]

*The saintly Henry VI
with his wife
Margaret of Anjou*

Whilst lauding Henry's supposed goodness, this panegyric does not suggest a man well suited to the rigours of medieval leadership and, further, it ought to be viewed in the light of Henry's potential candidacy for canonisation after his death in 1471. What is more, his obsession with chastity, which appears to have manifested itself in excessive prudery, suggests a degree of narrow minded instability that foreshadowed his later mental breakdown. He has generally been viewed as a failed monarch, an unworldly and weak-minded sovereign, prone to being manipulated by both his determined consort and his avaricious courtiers. It must be said that the economic challenge facing the Crown at the outset of Henry's reign, followed by a steadily deteriorating financial position, would have tested the determination of even the most dynamic monarch. During the reign of Richard II the annual income of the crown stood at around £120,000; by the 1450s this had declined sharply to no more than £40,000 [11]. To speak plainly, the royal purse was empty and the Crown virtually bankrupt.

In part Henry was culpable, in that he failed to manage his household expenses. However, due to factors beyond his control his core revenue was also plummeting: the yield from crown lands had tumbled and the level of income from customs and subsidies had dwindled. A slump in agriculture and a trade recession, which had begun to bite from the 1350s, fuelled the economic collapse. The King was not the only one to suffer: the same decline threatened also to impoverish the magnates, and it has been suggested that the financial pressures created by recession prompted the lords to compete more vigorously for Crown appointments [12].

Some of the nobility avoided falling into this trap by building up their holdings through judicious marriages and fortuitous inheritance: the Duke of York, the Duke of Buckingham and the Earl of Warwick all fit into this category. Such magnates tackled the loss of income from individual holdings by increasing the overall number of estates they owned.

By contrast, in the north of England the Percy family, once the over-mightiest of subjects, spent the early years of the fifteenth century trying to claw back what they had lost through earlier treasons. An agricultural slump in the years 1438-1440 caused yields to fall still further and exacerbated the Percies' burgeoning rivalry with the Nevilles. This dispute was to have a telling impact on the descent into lawlessness and, ultimately, civil war after 1453. One suggested cause of the Wars of the Roses was not that magnates were recruiting more soldiers (through the contract system described in the third part of this book) but that they could not afford to pay those already in their employment! [13]

A king who was weak financially would always face a harder task in controlling the great magnates than did one who enjoyed a more substantial income, especially as the same fiscal pressure was pushing the nobles to demand ever-larger slices of the diminishing cake of royal patronage. It was doubly unfortunate that the decline in the finances of the Crown should arrive at a time when the burden of maintaining the War in France was becoming well-nigh intolerable. Pressure on Crown finances exacerbated poor relations with the lords who had disbursed substantial amounts from their own stretched revenue to underwrite the government's obligations. Leading magnates such as John Talbot, Earl of Shrewsbury, struggled to recover monies they had laid out for the upkeep of garrisons in Normandy. The King's chronic indebtedness further damaged his standing amongst his lords and bound him deeper in a cycle of obligations which he could never hope to meet in full. After 1435 and the collapse of the Anglo-Burgundian entente, English fortunes in France, already wavering, began rapidly to decline. The next eighteen years saw a steadily mounting spate of losses, enlivened now and then by isolated successes.

The situation worsened in 1450, just a few years after the Treaty of Tours. Normandy, the vast patrimony that Henry V had taken and bequeathed to his son, was lost; the French reoccupied Normandy in a lightning campaign, the abusive English having lost the battle for the 'hearts and minds' of the local inhabitants. The shock provoked a constitutional crisis in England, and no amount of prayer on Henry's part could compensate for such national loss and humiliation.

Whether the ending of the war in 1453 might have acted as a further destabilising event is also relevant. An external war served to channel the aggressive tendencies of the magnates, provided fuel for martial hunger and, when victories mounted, raised the status of the Crown. Those who had participated in, or even remembered, the triumphal days of Henry V would find it hard to swallow the sorry tale of retreat and reversal that characterised his son's reign. William Worcester, chronicler and secretary to Sir John Fastolff, one of that dwindling band of grizzled veterans whose careers and fortunes had been made in the wars, lamented the death of chivalric opportunity [14].

To the national woe was added private quarrel. The resentment between John Beaufort, Duke of Somerset and Richard, Duke of York added bile to the political differences of the rival factions. York perceived Somerset to be incompetent; someone who had gained the post of Governor-General in 1447 without military credentials. This meant that York, who though lacking in brilliance was diligent and competent, was effectively sidelined during the campaigns in Normandy. Somerset went on to preside over the loss of the territory, thereby being branded both negligent and incapable. This also resulted in York losing a number of personal connections that he had built up in the province, at a time when his previous expenses were still unpaid. York was not the only loser; those of his faction who had served in Normandy also found themselves excluded after its loss in 1450. Those who had attached themselves to Somerset, including the Earl of Shrewsbury and the Lords Roos and Scales, fared better. In effect a quarrel that began in Normandy festered in England when that province was lost.

Although the loss of Normandy was tangible and humiliating, Somerset's perceived incompetence at least handed his rival a propaganda gift of rare value: it would be Somerset alone who was to blame for the final defeat, for the shameful and ignominious undoing of all that Henry V had established. This reversal of fortune was particularly resented in the South East, where the coastal counties lost the vital buffer of Normandy, a loss which allowed the renewal of amphibious raids by French privateers.

Somerset and the court faction had another cause for concern: Henry VI was still childless, his chaste disposition and his particular distaste for the lures of the flesh may well have been a contributing factor. A king without an heir was vulnerable and was failing in his dynastic duty. This weakness was exacerbated by the fact that, should Henry die childless, York was heir presumptive – equally telling, his direct claim to the throne was undeniable. Even if York was expressing no ambition in this respect so far, the threat hung around Somerset's neck, a leaden ghost of ambition [15].

Henry IV (Henry Bolingbroke) had usurped the throne in 1399 on the strength of his connection to Edward III, his grandfather, through his father John of Gaunt, Duke of Lancaster. However, Edward III had five sons altogether, and John was only the third eldest. Edward III's first son was another Edward, the Black Prince father of Richard II. The second son was Lionel, Duke of Clarence. The two sons younger than John of Gaunt were Edmund, Duke of York and Thomas of Woodstock.

Edmund Duke of York had a son, Richard, Earl of Cambridge, who married Anne Mortimer. This Richard was executed in 1415 for plotting against Henry V but not before he and Anne had a son themselves, naming him Richard. It was this last Richard, the son of an executed, treasonous man, who became Richard Duke of York, commander in Normandy and political enemy of John Beaufort, 1st Duke of Somerset.

Richard of York's claim to the throne was so strong because he was descended from the old King Edward III in two different ways. As we have read, he was descended from Edward on his father's side through Edmund, of York – Edward's fourth son. However, he was also descended from Edward III on his mother, Anne's side. She was directly descended from Lionel, Duke of Clarence – Edward III's second son. This was all the more dangerous because the House of Lancaster usurped the throne by claiming royal blood through John of Gaunt, who was merely the *third* son of Edward III. Anne Mortimer – Richard's mother – had a far better claim, her grandfather, Lionel being the elder brother of John of Gaunt.

Confusing as it may seem, this double connection meant that in a time of dynastic trouble, with Henry VI unwilling or unable to produce a male heir, the 'House of York' was officially a threat to the 'House of Lancaster'. With the king childless, York could be seen as waiting in the wings with the dream of a crown to spur him on. Should Henry die and York become King, the rising sun of Somerset and his acolytes would be eclipsed.

Notes:

[1] David II of Scotland was captured at the Battle of Neville's Cross, beneath Aldin Grange Bridge. Although badly wounded by arrows he still managed to knock out a couple of his captor's teeth before yielding!

[2] Gaunt also had dynastic ambitions in Spain by right of his wife Blanche of Castile; the lure of a foreign crown diverted his attention from the mounting difficulties of his nephew's reign.

[3] Seward D, *'Henry V as Warlord'* London 1987 pp.38-41

[4] The epic duel between Hotspur and Henry, whom the former had mentored and which Shakespeare creates as the climax to Henry IV Part 1, never took place. Henry was struck in the face by an arrow and injured quite early on in the fight. Hotspur, unwisely raising his own visor, was struck fully in the head and died.

[5] 'Bouches Inutiles' – literally 'useless mouths'. It was not uncommon for a hard-pressed commander to expel from a besieged town those who were

incapable of playing an active role in the defence, invariably the very young and the old, the sick and the lame. Henry refused passage through the lines for these wretched refugees, who were left to rot in No Man's Land.

[6] John Stewart Earl of Buchan (d.1424) was the son of Robert, Duke of Albany, a younger son of Robert II and *de facto* ruler of Scotland for most of his brother's reign. Widely believed to have been instrumental in the death of his nephew the Duke of Rothesay, Albany became regent when the young James I was kidnapped by English privateers and kept captive for many years. The regent appeared to be in no hurry to ransom his nephew and held sway until he was a ripe old age! The war with Donald of the Isles which culminated in the Battle of Harlaw, 1411, came about largely because of Albany's intention to confer the Earldom of Ross on Buchan rather than Donald, who believed, with some justification, that he had the better claim.

[7] This was the so-called 'Battle of the Herrings' in which the English force comprised the strong guard for a supply column and a substantial portion of these victuals comprised salted herring.

[8] Gillingham J, *Wars of the Roses* London 1981 pp.53-54

[9] Seward op. cit. p.41

[10] Gillingham op. cit. pp.53-54

[11] Pollard p.55

[12] Ibid. p.54

[13] Ibid. p.54

[14] Ibid. p.57

[15] York had been only four years of age when his father was executed, his uncle Edward, Duke of York, died in the press at Agincourt and Edmund Mortimer, Earl of March, of natural causes, a decade later. His material inheritance was very considerable and the residual claim of the Mortimer line came with it.

PART FIVE

THE UNQUIET PEACE

On 24 August 1453, Thomas Percy, Lord Egremont, younger son of the 2nd Earl of Northumberland, lay in ambush by Heworth Moor, north-east of York. With him were perhaps a thousand men at arms and archers; their intended quarry was the bridal party attending Sir Thomas Neville and his new wife, Maud Stanhope. The bride and groom were accompanied by Sir Thomas' parents, the Earl and Countess of Salisbury, with Thomas' brother John, the future Lord Montagu.

All were travelling north from Tattershall Castle in Lincolnshire where the marriage had been celebrated. The Nevilles were neither unguarded nor unaware and, when the Percy men swarmed from their ambush, the bridal party acquitted themselves more than adequately and the attack was vigorously repulsed. Although on the surface this affair may appear to have been little more than a local brawl, it could be said to represent the first major armed clash of the Wars of the Roses. Some commentators have also interpreted the Percy v Neville feud as the catalyst which led mere factionalism to degenerate into civil war. Regardless of the details of their involvement, both parties were active in the wider movement to reform and ultimately remove the Lancastrian administration [1].

As a local dynasty the rise of the Percies had been meteoric. In the early 14th Century the family held no land in Northumberland. It was Henry Percy I who purchased the manor of Alnwick (so many men of the Percy line were christened 'Henry' that they were numbered, like royalty. In the north the comparison was a valid one). Henry I bought the manor for £5,000 from the Prince Bishop, Anthony Bek, not withstanding the fact that the Bishop's title may have been defective [2]. Henry Percy II extended his holdings in the county and, in 1327, contracted with the young King Edward II to act as lieutenant on the borders, in consideration of an annual fee of 500 marks. Subsequently, Henry Percy III traded this annuity for a reversionary interest in the Clavering estate of Warkworth and further purchased Corbridge, Newburn and Rothbury.

An important local aspect of the years 1330-1400 was the toll taken on the gentry of Northumberland by the Scottish wars. Power and influence increasingly went to those who held Crown offices and who were best placed to profit from the unending strife. The cross border strife directly fuelled the seemingly inexorable rise of the Percy dynasty. In order to play his own dynastic game in France, Edward III needed strong local forces available on the frontier to resist the Scots; as wardens the Percies could raise and maintain forces at the Crown's expense, and along with the Nevilles, another up-and-coming family, they did not shirk their obligations: together they led an army which crushed an invading Scots force at Neville's Cross in 1346.

Henry Percy IV became the 1st Earl of Northumberland in 1377 and continued the process of acquisition as well as swapping some of his Yorkshire properties for the manors of Guyzance, Rennington, Shilbottle, Lucker, Swinhoe and Broxfield in 1395. Henry Percy V ('Hotspur') bought up Newham, Newstead, Ellingham and Byker. By 1400 the

Percies owned five baronies and no fewer than seventy one manors. The Percies' almost princely independence reached its zenith in the late 14th Century when Henry Percy IV and 'Hotspur' rebelled against an attempt by King Henry IV to curb their power. The rebellion ended in defeat; Hotspur died a traitor on the field of Shrewsbury in 1403, his land and titles were stripped from him and his family.

Into the resulting power vacuum stepped the Neville family, their success due, in part, to this Percy failure [3]. Under the steady, if grasping, hand of Ralph Neville, 1st Earl of Westmorland, the family gradually increased its estates and spheres of influence whilst remaining staunchly loyal to Henry IV and the House of Lancaster. This loyalty was conspicuously demonstrated when Ralph Neville died in 1425. His effigy (which can be seen in Staindrop Church, County Durham) shows him wearing the distinctive 'S' collar, the talisman of a solid Lancastrian [4].

*Effigy of
Ralph Neville
1364-1425
showing the 'S' collar
of a loyal Lancastrian.*

Ralph Neville, 1st Earl of Westmorland, cemented his relationship with the crown by marrying, as his second wife, Joan Beaufort, a daughter of John of Gaunt, Duke of Lancaster. This second marriage produced

Richard Neville, who became Earl of Salisbury (he was elevated to the earldom in 1429, having married Alice Monagu, the only daughter and heir of Thomas Montagu, Earl of Salisbury). Although his father had older children by his first wife, Richard inherited the bulk of the Neville holdings in Yorkshire, centred on the valuable estates of Middleham and Sheriff Hutton. The rest of the vast patrimony went to his half-brothers. The great worth of Richard's legacy sparked a deep division with his older half brothers and sisters, who retained the title and lands in the north-west but obviously felt entitled to Salisbury's lands too! Undisturbed by the family rift, Salisbury went on steadily to build up his holdings.

Richard Neville
16th Earl of Warwick
'The Kingmaker'
1428-1471

His own eldest son, another Richard Neville, added the dazzling Beauchamp inheritance and the earldom of Warwick to his titles and was to mature into a key figure on the political landscape. He brought great economic power and status to his name – 'Warwick the Kingmaker' – before crashing to ruin. Always something of a swashbuckler:

> … he had energy, dash and courage. A skilful propagandist, he had great success in rousing the common people to his cause and was well noted for his open handed generosity. Yet he was also self-interested and arrogant … acquisitive and unscrupulous to a degree … unusually ruthless in his treatment of defeated enemies [7].

The Beaufort clan, in the person of John Beaufort, 1st Duke of Somerset, was placed high in the Council of Henry VI and so the Neville allegiance seemed thriving and secure [5]. William Neville, Lord Fauconberg, ('Little Fauconberg'), together with others of the Neville affinity, George Lord Latimer, Edward Lord Abergavenny and his son Sir Thomas are consistently named in commissions of the peace. At various times Fauconberg, a veteran of the French and Scottish Wars, was Seneschal, Steward, Justice of Assize and Justice of Gaol Delivery. Latimer acted as chamberlain and Thomas also held similar offices to those of his uncle, including that of Commissioner of Array for the wards of Chester, Darlington, Easington and the Wapentake of Sadberge [6].

While the Nevilles were scaling the political ladder and feuding amongst themselves, Harry Hotpur's son, yet another Henry, was working towards reversing his father's attainder of 1403 (which he did in 1416) and then reclaiming his father's lost inheritance. This task took him from 1416-1440. Salisbury, therefore, as one of the most powerful members of the Neville family, had plenty of time to consolidate his hold on manors in Cleveland, Westmorland, Cumberland and the important lordship of Raby [8]. In this period the three ridings of Yorkshire were parcelled out between four of the greatest magnates of the realm: the Crown (as Duchy of Lancaster), Percies, Nevilles and the Duke of York who was also the Earl of Salisbury's brother in law. The Percy holdings, east of the Pennines, were interspersed with those of Salisbury and York, though the latter showed scant interest in his northern estates [9].

Salisbury's bickering with the senior branch of the Neville family continued over this period and even a negotiated settlement of 1443 did not appease the bitterness. Salisbury certainly could not depend on his kin to back him in a feud with the Percies [10]. In the same year he was appointed

Warden of the West March, a prestigious office. By the early 1440s his annual income could have reached the very substantial amount of £3,000, only £500 behind the Bishop of Durham, but perhaps as much as £1,000 more than Northumberland could garner [11]. After a decade in office, Salisbury retained his post, now held jointly with his son Warwick.

For decades the Percies had been active and pre-eminent in border affairs: Hotspur fought at the Battle of Otterburn in 1388 and the Battle of Homildon fourteen years later against the Scots. The 2nd Earl of Northumberland's second son, Henry Percy, Lord Poynings, also held the East March wardenry from 1440. The office of Warden, which had its origins in the earlier medieval period, was well established by the mid 15th Century, with the power and burden of the holder clearly defined. These obligations included, *inter alia*, the holding of the monthly truce days with the Warden's opposite number on the Scottish side, gleaning intelligence, maintaining the watch, garrisoning strongpoints, pursuing raiders (over the frontier if need be) and leading retaliatory strikes or 'warden rodes' [12].

Having enjoyed the privileges of the wardenry for so long the Percies tended to rely on the robust thuggery of Border practice. In January 1453, an incident involving a band of Percy tenants in the manor of Topcliffe demonstrated that they were confident that no sheriff or other Crown official could wield power enough to impose the rule of law as opposed to the rule of the Percies, and this state of affairs held for all areas in which the Percies held sway. This aggressive posturing was fed by the conduct of Lord Egremont, Thomas Percy, younger son of the 2nd Earl of Northumberland. Egremont had threatened the life of the Sheriff of Cumberland, Thomas de la Mare, an adherent of Richard Neville, Earl of Salisbury [13].

Egremont, who had gained his lordship in 1449 at the age of twenty five, typified all the adverse traits of his name: 'quarrelsome, violent and contemptuous of all authority, he possessed all the worst characteristics of a Percy for which his grandfather is still a byword' [14]. Salisbury's sister, Eleanor, was married to Henry Percy, 2nd Earl of Northumberland, but the ties of blood counted for little in a game with such high stakes. Both families possessed mature and ambitious patriarchs, each with a brood of young, restless and potentially lawless sons, and no shortage of available manpower [15].

When Thomas Neville married Maud Stanhope, this proved a provocation too far for the volatile Egremont. The bride had been married before, to Robert, Lord Willoughby of Eresby, who had died the previous summer. She was also the niece and co-heiress of Ralph, Lord Cromwell, an ill tempered character who had acquired the leases on two choice manors at Wressle and Burwell in Lincolnshire. These had previously been in the hands of the Percies, but in February 1440, Lord Cromwell had purchased the reversionary interest and the Earl of Northumberland, whose family had spent lavishly on Wressle, had litigated in vain. Thus, when Cromwell married his niece to a Neville he was adding insult to injury [16]. Tension had been mounting throughout the early summer of 1452 and in June Henry VI summoned Thomas Percy, Lord Egremont and John Neville, Lord Montagu (younger brother of Richard Neville, Earl of Warwick) to be before him by the end of that month. Neville did not attend, being too busy laying plans for an ambush of his own.

Henry, having dissolved parliament on 2 July, journeyed north to confront his quarrelsome vassals. He proposed that Percy and his affinity should gird themselves in readiness for service in Gascony, where their martial spirit might be more usefully deployed. However, the proposal

CR

King Henry VI
1421-1471

came to nothing. On 12 July the King established a commission of oyer and terminer, the membership of which included the rival earls and some fourteen others [17]. A fortnight later, the commission was re-issued but to little effect. Richard Neville, Earl of Salisbury, sat in the Council (unlike Henry Percy, Earl of Northumberland) and undoubtedly used his influence to pack the membership with allies, Neville stalwarts such as Sir James Pickering, Sir Henry Fitzhugh and Sir Henry le Scrope of Bolton [18].

Despite the commission's excellent credentials it proved ineffective amidst a rising tide of disorder. By the end of July, a new and perhaps less overtly partisan body was set up under the guidance of Sir William Lucy, a knight of Northamptonshire and a Council member. Immediately Sir William set to work, summoning Ralph Neville, Sir John Conyers, Sir James Pickering, Sir Ralph Randolf, Sir Thomas Mountford, Richard Aske, Thomas Sewer and John Alcombe. On 10 August nine Percy adherents were summoned, together with both Sir Ralph and Sir Richard Percy [19], although yet again with little result.

By this point, Thomas Percy, Lord Egremont was preparing for the ambush which took place on 24 August 1453 by Heworth Moor, north east of York. York was the economic and cultural capital of the north, equally important to both Nevilles and Percies. The city, as a major mercantile centre, was suffering from the general recession of the 1450s and from the loss of Gascony which had seriously affected the all-important wine trade (which for three hundred years was based in Bordeaux). The North Sea was infested with pirates, relations with the Hanse were difficult and the diminished English hopes in France only worsened the situation [20]. Recession and unemployment provided a reservoir of available manpower which could be drawn into the Percy/Neville feud. Of the 710 people named on indictments for the ambush laid before the Duke of York the following summer, some 94% were northern gentry and yeomen; slightly more than 15% were citizens of York [21]

Undeterred by the failure on Heworth Moor, Sir Richard Percy (younger brother of Henry and Thomas) and a band of unruly adherents now embarked on a spree of vandalism, culminating in the kidnapping of Lawrence Catterall, the bailiff of Staincliff Wapentake. Catterall was dragged roughly from his devotions in Gargrave Church on 9 September and incarcerated, first in Isel Castle and then in Cockermouth. Obviously the luckless man had, in some unrecorded way, offended the Percies [22]. The unrest continued; on 25 September a brace of Percy retainers, John Catterall and Sir John Salvin, pillaged the house of William Hebdon, vicar of Aughton. This may have been in reprisal for John Neville's plundering of the Earl of Northumberland's property at Catton [23].

On 8 October 1453, King Henry wrote plaintively to both earls, enjoining them to exercise some degree of control over their headstrong offspring. At this time the King's mental health was already causing concern: the exact nature of his malady has never been definitively diagnosed, although catatonic schizophrenia has been favoured by some commentators. Whatever the cause, the plain fact was that Henry's deteriorating mental condition contributed to his loosening grip on his administration and on law and order in the North.

By 17 October, Thomas Percy, Lord Egremont had assembled perhaps fifty harnessed retainers who mustered at Topcliffe, rather fewer than half of whom were from the Percy heartland of Northumberland or from the City of Newcastle [24]. Ignoring any feeble royal admonitions, both sides were squaring up for a further brawl and an actual confrontation probably occurred at Sandhutton a few days later on 20 October.

Seal of Richard Neville
Earl of Salisbury
1400-1460

Here, Richard Neville, Earl of Salisbury and his son Richard Neville, Earl of Warwick, joined by Sir John Neville, Lord Montagu and Sir Thomas Neville, were bolstered by such trusty friends as Sir Henry Fitzhugh and Sir Henry le Scrope. Not to be outdone the Percy affinity was led by Henry Percy, 2nd Earl of Northumberland, his son, Henry Percy, Lord Poynings, Thomas Percy, Lord Egremont and Sir Richard Percy. The stand-off seems to have amounted to little more than bravado on both sides but the magnates themselves had clearly shown their hands in the fracas: battle lines had been drawn, even if very few blows had yet been struck [25].

As the tempo of strife rose the King's grasp on reality declined and it had, by now, become impossible to hide the fact of his condition. Matters were further stirred by the birth on 13 October of a son, Edward of Lancaster. With this, Richard Duke of York's hopes of securing the succession from a childless monarch vanished into the mist. Increasingly vociferous,

Richard of York was clamouring to be appointed as regent during the term of the King's illness, a demand that York's rival the Duke of Somerset was determined to resist. On 25 October the Council convened at York with Salisbury and Warwick in attendance. Both Northumberland and Lord Poynings were pointedly absent [26]. The Duke of York had married Salisbury's sister, Cicely, the celebrated 'Rose of Raby', making Salisbury and York brothers-in-law. As a man Richard of York was:

> ... a somewhat austere, remote and unsympathetic figure, with little capacity of inclination to seek out and win support from his fellow noblemen or from the wider public [27].

Richard
Duke of York
c.1410-1460

When the King's mental health finally gave way, Somerset could not stand up to York and his powerful Neville allies. On 27 March 1454 York was formally installed as Protector, charged with ruling England on behalf of Prince Edward while his father remained incapacitated. Salisbury was made Chancellor. No sooner was York in office than his former rival Edmund Beaufort, 2nd Duke of Somerset, was consigned to a sojourn in the Tower [28]. Richard Neville, Earl of Warwick also had Beaufort blood, from his grandmother Joan Beaufort, but this didn't stop him supporting Somerset's fall. Warwick had maintained a separate quarrel with Somerset, over title to a portion of his vast inheritance. Somerset's greed had surpassed his judgement, making an enemy of the Earl of Warwick.

With the Nevilles now so firmly aligned with the Yorkist faction, it was probably inevitable that the Percies would gravitate towards Somerset's party, despite its present eclipse. In this way the local rivalry between Percy and Neville was subsumed into the greater antipathy between York and Somerset, which ultimately became York and Lancaster.

In May 1454 York, as Protector, sent a strongly worded summons to the Earl of Northumberland, ordering him to appear before the Council on 12 June. Lord Poynings and Ralph Percy were summoned to appear ten days before this. Already, on 3 April, Henry Holand, 3rd Duke of Exeter who had sought common cause with the Percies in an earlier dispute, was removed from his lucrative and prestigious post of Lord Admiral [29]. Unsurprisingly, the Percies were not minded to follow the path of humility. On 6 May, they showed what respect they had for the new Chancellor Salisbury by vandalising his house in York and 'roughing up' one of his tenants, John Skipworth. Many of those involved in this fresh rash of disturbances had been 'out' upon Heworth Moor the previous summer.

By the middle of May, Thomas Percy, Lord Egremont was mustering his affinity at Spofforth in North Yorkshire and there, on the 14 May, he was joined by Henry Holand, Duke of Exeter, bridling at the humiliation of his demotion from the office of Admiral. Riotous behaviour broke out in the streets of York, alarming the burgesses, especially after the mob had brutally assaulted the Mayor and the Recorder. A wave of anarchy now swept through the North Riding, whilst Exeter, not to be outdone, busily stirred up trouble in Lancashire and Cheshire [30].

Needless to say the invigorated Council, supported by York as Protector, did not sit idle. Sir Thomas Stanley, the Duchy of Lancaster's Receiver

Thomas Stanley
1st Earl of Derby
c.1435-1504

for the counties of Lancashire and Cheshire, ably assisted by Sir Thomas Harrington, saw Exeter off in short order. The Protector himself entered the City of York on 19 May – the rioters fled the streets [31]. Exeter, whose thuggish traits matched those of Egremont, was, nonetheless, one of King Henry's closest blood relations, tracing his line through John of Gaunt. It is conceivable that he perceived, in this localised brawl, the chance to light a fuse that might unseat York and see him appointed in his stead [32]. On 21 May, with Egremont and his affinity, he reappeared in York and set about further intimidation of the much abused Mayor and burgesses. Disorder flared up once again throughout the shire.

While these events were occurring, the Council in London dispatched a message of protest to the Scots regarding a completely separate incident – a violation of a truce the previous year. The Exeter and Egremont contigent kidnapped the herald who was carrying this message of protest to Scotland! This smacked of rebellion and the rebels, as they could now be termed, planned to lure York the Protector into an ambush beneath the walls of the northern capital [33].

York summoned both of the ringleaders, Egremont and Exeter, to appear before him on 25 June 1454. He used the time running up to that date to consolidate his position and to build up local forces. By 15 June, York was reinforced by Warwick, Lord Greystoke, Lord Clifford, the Earl of

Shrewsbury, Sir Henry Fitzhugh and all their retinues. On the due date of 25 June, Exeter, Egremont as well as Sir Richard Percy all failed to appear [34]. For all their violent posturing the rebels had completely failed to achieve any serious objective. Exeter crept back to London and by 8 July he was in captivity. By 24 July he had been safely incarcerated in Pontefract Castle. York stayed in the North, not secure enough to return to the capital with the Percies still at large [35].

Matters continued in this tense vein until the autumn when a further confrontation took place, this time at Stamford Bridge; heavy with ancient blood this was some miles east of York and held by the Nevilles. Whether any actual fighting occurred is doubtful, but the Percy faction was confounded by treachery: Peter Lound, one of their own bailiffs, deserted with some two hundred followers. The Nevilles, led by Thomas and John, pounced on their discomfited enemies and captured both Egremont and Sir Richard Percy. The prisoners were sent, probably via Middleham, to Newgate Gaol and were arraigned before the Protector, the Duke of York, on 4 November. Both were penalised by the imposition of onerous fines: Salisbury was to be compensated to the sum of 8,000 marks, and other members of the Neville clan were awarded lesser amounts. The total burden was some 16,800 marks, an indebtedness the Percies could not hope to discharge straight away and, as was no doubt intended, they remained behind bars [36].

If the Nevilles felt they had cause for satisfaction their triumph was short-lived, for in December 1454 Henry VI recovered his wits and was deemed able to resume the reins of government. The office of Protector was made redundant on 7 February and the Duke of Somerset was freed from the Tower, reinstated to all of his many offices. A month later the Earl of Salisbury bowed to the inevitable, and resigned as Chancellor. A mere seven days after his incarceration Henry Holand, Duke of Exeter was set at liberty. Somerset, along with the Queen – who had seen her husband treated with disdain – was in the mood for retribution rather than for compromise. A further trial of strength now appeared inevitable.

On 22 May 1455, the opposing factions clashed bloodily in the streets of St Albans. Here Edmund Beaufort, 2nd Duke of Somerset, Henry Percy 2nd Earl of Northumberland and Lord Clifford, choked out their life blood on the cobbles. War had been declared. The Somerset faction and those loyal to the House of Lancaster were defeated; the hapless King Henry was left as a puppet of the victorious Yorkists.

On 31 July, York issued a general amnesty, though if he imagined this would scour the blood of the fallen from the streets of St Albans, he was very much in error. Battle lines had been drawn, blood feuds engendered. The younger generation of Lancastrian Lords, Henry Beaufort 3rd Duke of Somerset, Henry Percy 3rd Earl of Northumberland and John de Clifford 13th Baron Clifford had all lost their fathers and they thirsted for vengeance.

During the uncertain months of the winter of 1455-1456, further disturbances broke out in the North, largely orchestrated by Thomas Percy, Lord Egremont, who had escaped from Newgate Gaol on 13 November. Further aggrieved by the spilling of Percy blood, he occupied Wressle, that contentious jewel, (which was finally granted to him in 1458). By 14 January 1456, Henry Holand, Duke of Exeter, imprisoned once again after St Albans, was at liberty and ripe for mischief, plotting with the Earl of Shrewsbury and the Duke of Somerset to assassinate Warwick in November 1456.

King Henry, with the conciliatory Duke of Buckingham, attempted to broker an accord. This resulted in the near farcical sham of 'Love-Day' on 25 March 1458, where both sides entered into bonds for mutual damages and absolved each other and their affinities of the blood debt. This was no more than a lull, a sham papering over cracks that soon yawned wide. By the following year Queen Margaret, now the driving force behind the court faction, was firmly in control of the English polity: when a council meeting was proposed at Coventry in June 1459, York, Salisbury and Warwick were excluded.

Salisbury, at this time, was at his estate of Middleham and his son Warwick was in the capital. York asked both of them to journey to his base at Ludlow. As the elder Neville, Richard Earl of Salisbury, made his way to Ludlow on 23 September 1459, a force of Lancastrians, under Lord Audley, barred his road at Blore Heath, near Newcastle under Lyme. A battle ensued and the Yorkists, though outnumbered, took the field, leaving Audley and many others dead or dying.

In spite of this fresh victory, the next confrontation, which occurred at Ludford Bridge the following month, went badly wrong for the Yorkists.

The Rout

Andrew Trollope, one of York's affinity, an officer of the Calais garrison and a seasoned veteran, defected with his entire company, fatally compromising the position. York and the others suffered a collective loss of nerve and took flight, abandoning their following.

The Duke of York, and his younger son, Edmund, Earl of Rutland made for Ireland. The Eark of Warwick, together with his father the Earl of Salisbury and York's eldest son Edward, Earl of March headed for Calais; Warwick was still a nominal Captain of Calais and expected some degree of safety there. A Lancastrian assembly known to the Yorkists as the 'Parliament of Devils' attainted the scattered rebels.

It is possible to sense a resulting shift of power within the Yorkist affinity. The aggressive younger generation of Warwick and March began to flex their muscles; after conferring with York in Ireland in March 1460, Warwick planned a renewed offensive. This was a brilliant success. On 26 June 1460 he landed at Sandwich in Kent, which was then a major port. His popularity in the south-east of the country was considerable: vigorous naval patrolling had scoured the Channel of pirates and privateers alike and he had filled the harbour at Calais with his prizes – captured ships which were sold along with their cargoes. The Yorkists first took London before meeting the King's army at Northampton on 10 July. The Duke of Buckingham and Lord Egremont both fell and the Yorkists won the day. Henry VI became a prisoner.

In September 1460 the Duke of York returned to London, making it plain that he was no longer interested in acting as a mere Protector – he had come to assert his right to the throne itself. This was a political blunder which alienated the majority of the magnates who were not yet receptive to régime change. Warwick, angered and alarmed, appeared to be wrong footed by his uncle's political ineptitude.

CR

Margaret of Anjou
1430-1482

On 24 October Parliament attempted to enact a form of compromise: the Act of Accord secured Henry's throne for his lifetime but passed the succession to York. This of course outraged the Queen, Margaret of Anjou, whose son Edward would thereby lose his inheritance. The Act of Accord arguably transformed the war from a factional struggle into a dynastic one; the stakes had just been raised. It could also be said that the conflict became regionalised, North versus South. In the North the Queen found her greatest support where the 3rd Earl of Northumberland, Lord Clifford, Lord Greystoke and Lord Neville (of the Westmorland branch) attended a muster held in either Hull or at Pontefract. The tide of resentment swelled and Margaret soon found herself in command of a predominantly northern army.

To meet this new threat, York, together with his younger son the Earl of Rutland and the Earl of Salisbury, marched from London in December 1460 with only slender forces, unaware of the extent of the Lancastrian threat. York celebrated what was to be his last Christmas at his castle of Sandal, near Wakefield. On 30 December, probably lured out by a ruse, his vastly inferior forces engaged those of the Queen, now under the overall command of Henry Beaufort, 3rd Duke of Somerset. York fell in the disastrous Battle of Wakefield, along with Sir Thomas Neville. York's young son Edmund, Earl of Rutland, was also cut down by John de Clifford – a murder which earned him his sobriquet 'The Butcher'. Salisbury was taken and incarcerated briefly at Pontefract but he was discovered by the commoners, who dragged him out to his death.

Micklegate Bar at York

The heads of executed traitors were displayed here as a deterrent to others of the same mind. The heads of Sir Henry Percy, the Duke of York and the Earl of Northumberland all ended up here, skewered on pike-staffs and left to rot.

In Shakespeare's Henry VI, Queen Margaret commands: 'Off with his head and set it on York gates; so York may overlook the town of York', after which the head of the duke found its place here.

Flush with victory, the heads of their fallen foes impaled above Micklegate in York, Queen Margaret's host swept southward, descending on the unprotected lowlands with biblical fury. The *boreales bobinantes* (literally, 'roaring northerners'), were not well liked – their path, according to the chroniclers, being marked by rapine and plunder. The Earl of Warwick advanced from the capital and dug in by St Albans to meet this intimidating host. Unfortunately for Warwick, at the second battle of St Albans on 2 February 1461, he was outflanked and outfought. He was badly mauled and deprived of the captive King Henry who had been carted in his train.

Comfort, for the Yorkists, came from the west. York's elder son, Edward Earl of March, had been leading a blocking force into the Welsh marches, seeking to stop Welsh Lancastrians linking forces with the Queen. In this, March was successful, snatching a dazzling victory at Mortimer's Cross, also in February 1461. Now reunited, the King and Queen recoiled from an assault on London, where sentiment ran high against them and their rapacious northerners.

Edward IV
1442-1483

This kind of fear was a useful propaganda tool for Warwick who decided to take action and put forward the Duke of York's eldest son Edward as the next King of England. On 4 March the eighteen year old rode into Westminster, where he assumed the crown as King Edward IV. The realm now had two sovereigns.

By now the Lancastrian tide was ebbing northwards, retreating into Yorkshire behind the formidable barrier of the River Aire. Neither of the two kings could be secure until he had defeated the other in open field, and the Duke of Norfolk was dispatched to his native East Anglia to raise fresh forces whilst Warwick did the same in the midlands. On 11 March,

William Neville, Lord Fauconberg led the Yorkist van out of London; Edward followed soon after. On a gentle plateau that swells between the villages of Towton and Saxton, the Duke of Somerset deployed his considerable army, perhaps 30,000 or more. With him was the Duke of Exeter, the Earl of Northumberland, Lord Clifford, Ralph Lord Dacre of Gilsland and Andrew Trollope who had defected before the rout of Ludford Bridge. Thus, the stage was set for, arguably, the biggest land battle ever to be fought in Great Britain.

In the biting sleet of a bitter Palm Sunday 1461, the Battle of Towton was fought – a long, vicious and exceedingly bloody struggle. By the end of that dreadful day the Lancastrians were utterly defeated, though the issue was long in doubt. The flower of the North, including Northumberland, Dacre and Clifford, perished alongside thousands of the commons. Such a titanic defeat should have marked the end of this phase of the wars, but it did not. The remaining Lancastrians fled to the North, their cause kept alive in the county of Northumberland. Three more long and wearying years of war lay ahead.

Notes:

[1] Griffiths R A, 'Local Rivalries and National Politics: The Percies, the Nevilles and the Duke of Exeter, 1452-1455' Speculum vol. XLIII 1968 p.589
[2] Watson G, 'The Border Reivers' Newcastle upon Tyne 1974 pp.139-149
[3] Weiss H, 'A Power in the North? The Percies in the Fifteenth Century' The Historical Journal 19.2 1965 pp.501-509
[4] Pollard p.42

[5] Ross C, 'The Wars of the Roses' London 1976 p.31

[6] Weiss op. cit. p.504

[7] Ross op. cit. p.31

[8] Griffiths op. cit. p590

[9] Ibid. p.589

[10] Ibid. p.591

[11] Ibid. p.593

[12] Tough D L W, 'Last Years of a Frontier' Oxford 1928 pp.77-87

[13] Griffiths op. cit. p.592

[14] Ibid. p.591

[15] Ibid. p.592

[16] Ibid. p.594

[17] Ibid. p.594

[18] Ibid. p.595

[19] Ibid. p.595

[20] Seward D, 'The Wars of the Roses' London 1995 pp. 23-25

[21] Griffiths op. cit. p.592

[22] Ibid. p.602

[23] Ibid. p.603

[24] Ibid. p.604

[25] Ibid. p.605

[26] Ibid. p.605

[27] Ross op. cit. p.28

[28] Ibid. p.29

[29] Griffiths op. cit. p.610

[30] Ibid. p.611

[31] Ibid. p.612

[32] Ibid. p.613

[33] Ibid. p.616

[34] Ibid. p.620

PART SIX

WAR IN THE NORTH

The Act of Attainder, passed by Edward IV's victorious Parliament, attainted all of the northern lords who had fallen in the battle of Towton: The Earl of Northumberland, the Lords Clifford, Neville and Dacre and many others from the region including Sir Humphrey Dacre, Sir Thomas Findern, Sir John Heron, Sir Henry Bellingham, Sir Robert Whittingham, Sir Ralph Randolf, Robert Bellingham of Westmorland, Thomas Stanley, John Smothing, Robert Bolling, Robert Hatecale, Richard Everingham, Richard Cokerell, (these last five from York), Roger Wharton from Westmorland and Rauf Chernok from Lancashire.

Although the Lancastrians had been grievously defeated, the Milanese ambassador to the court of Charles VII, Prospero di Camulio, writing soon after the battle, sounded a cautious note:

'[I]f the King and Queen of England with the other fugitives mentioned above are not taken, it seems certain that in time fresh disturbances will arise' [1].

This observation was to prove grimly prophetic as the focus of the war moved northwards into Northumberland, where it was to fester for

91

CR

Edward IV
1442-1483

the next three years. The county of Northumberland was a very different region from North Yorkshire where the troubles of the preceding decade and the battles between 1459 and 1461 took place. There is perhaps a tendency amongst historians to point generally to the 'North' as though the land north of the Trent were a single region. This is not the case today, nor was it in the 15th Century. The cultural, topographical and social fabric of the north embraced 'a kaleidoscope of overlapping regions and localities' [2].

Northumberland is the most northerly of the English counties and it shares a long border with Scotland. England and Scotland had been at war, if not continuously then certainly on a regular footing, since 1296. During these years, even when open hostilities were not in progress there continued a rumbling of low intensity warfare on the border, based around cattle raiding and centred on the upland dales of Northumberland, Liddesdale, Teviotdale, the Merse and much of the West.

Northumberland also has a very long coastline, with sweeping stretches of white sands facing the cold passage of the North Sea. To the south it is hemmed by the waters of Tyne and to the north, the North Pennines. These border hills rise to the shoulder of the Cheviot Massif, a bare haunch of heather and peat bog, slashed by the upland dales of the Coquet, Aln, Breamish and Till. Although still heavily wooded in parts, the rich soils of these valleys were heavily farmed [3].

The fortresses of Dunstanburgh and Bamburgh, which featured heavily in the northern war, both occupy outcrops of the same dolerite upon which Hadrian's Wall rests. In the west of the county, the valleys of the North Tyne and Rede bisect the uplands. A fertile plain to the south and east of the county curls around the high moorland and the mix of soil and clay here is ideally suited to husbandry [4]. In the late medieval period, village fields in the area were often surrounded by common or waste and substantial tracts of woodland, such as those around Rothbury and Brinkburn. Large spaces were also set aside for lordly deer parks, such as those near Alnwick or Felton.

Though arable farming predominated in the lowland areas, with oats and wheat as the staple crops, pastoral farming was equally important. The animals grazed on common or fallow land with the higher pastures used in the summer. For all Northumbrians there was an omnipresent menace of reivers, who were a product of Edward III's early victories in Scotland, after which he populated the buffer zone or 'Pale' between the two countries with a tough breed of settlers, more

Edward III
1312-1377

proficient with the sword than with the plough. By the 1450s a culture of cross border cattle raiding, theft and feuding between rival families was the norm. The reivers were most active in the autumn, at a time of year when the secret ways over the mosses and high moorland were dry and navigable and the shortening days afforded the greater cloak of darkness [5]. Life in the county was thus essentially rural and agrarian, and by the early 14th Century the pattern of boroughs was established: Alnwick, Alnmouth, Bamburgh, Corbridge, Felton, Haltwhistle, Haydon Bridge, Hexham, Mitford, Morpeth, Newbiggin, Newbrough, Newcastle, Norham, Rothbury, Warkworth, Warenmouth and Wooler. Many of these were in coastal locations where fishing constituted the principal economic activity; others, such as Norham, Hexham and Corbridge, were sited at strategic river crossings. Only Newcastle, Morpeth and Alnwick were of any real size [6].

Newcastle was by far the largest settlement, a major provincial port but smaller than Bristol and York, York being the northern region's capital. Newcastle's importance was created by its long distance seaborne trade with the south of England and the continental North Sea ports. Its continued growth was funded by the expansion of coal mining in south east Northumberland. In keeping with the frontier status of the county, its principle town was still surrounded by a strong stone curtain wall, studded with eighteen towers and pierced by six fortified gateways [7].

Berwick upon Tweed, wrested from the Scots in a torrent of blood and passed back and forth for many decades, was a vital border bastion, much besieged by both sides. Its great walls and castle had been strengthened after the initial escalade in 1296, and added to in stages ever since [8]. A pattern of unremitting strife contributed to an embattled landscape and the coastline south of Berwick was covered with major forts at Tynemouth, Warkworth, Dunstanburgh and Bamburgh. Inland, castles or smaller fortalices guarded important river crossings: Alnwick and Prudhoe counted amongst these. Berwick, Norham and Wark (on Tweed) lined the eastern flank of the border with Scotland, whilst garrisons at Harbottle and Bewcastle existed to intercept the thieves' roads [9].

To the west of the Cheviots the picture was not dissimilar. Carlisle, with its great red sandstone Norman keep, had been the gateway to the English west for centuries; the keep had defied every assault – and there had been more than a few by the Scots. Carlisle was a flourishing inland port in its own right, with ships plying the busy routes to Ireland and the Isle of Man. Naworth and Askerton stood along the West March, an area the Scots frequently chose as an incursion route.

Alnwick Castle, major bastion against the Scots

A number of these fortifications were to prove significant in the struggles of 1461-1464 but none more so than the three great east coastal fortresses of Alnwick, Bamburgh and Dunstanburgh. Of these, Alnwick was a major bastion against the Scots which had defied successive attempts to take it [10]. It was the jewel of the Percies and much improved by them over several generations [11]. The site enclosed an area of some seven acres, in plan, a large shell keep rested on a levelled motte, which separated the east and west baileys (or courtyards). The donjon (or keep) was studded with seven semi-circular towers. The enceinte had been fortified with additional towers and a substantial gatehouse with a barbican.

Bamburgh, as previously noted, occupies a spur of the whin sill, rising 150' (46m) from the flat coastal plain. It was the ancient seat of the Northumbrian Kings and said to be the 'Joyous Garde' of Arthurian legend. The fortress encloses an area of some eight acres along the narrow ridge and has an inner, an eastern and a western bailey. The massive square keep dates from the 12th Century and both eastern and western gateways were heavily fortified [12].

Dunstanburgh Castle from the North

Begun by Thomas, Earl of Lancaster, Dunstanburgh also occupies a dolerite outcrop, much rebuilt in the 14th Century by John of Gaunt. On the north, the cliff falls sheer requiring no man-made works; curtain walls rose on the other three sides. The inner ward dates from Gaunt's time as does the tall mass of the fortified gatehouse, originally finished with a strong outwork or barbican. This arrangement was perceived as being inherently weak, and a more ingenious covered entrance towards the west was constructed [13].

After receiving the dire news of her defeat at Towton, Queen Margaret fled north into Scotland, dragging her husband and her young son Edward of Lancaster along with a scattering of survivors including Somerset, Roos, Exeter and Sir John Fortescue. Margaret possibly held the view that the Northumbrians were solidly Lancastrian, following the lead of the Percies who, as it has been argued 'have the hearts of the north and always have had' [14]. This may have been the case – whilst the Nevilles challenged the Percies in Durham and North Yorkshire they had little influence in this most northerly shire.

On 22 April 1461, some three weeks after Towton, King Edward IV progressed northward to Newcastle, where on 1 May he attended the execution of James Butler, Earl of Wiltshire. Having established his authority, the King soon tired of the North, and with pressing matters awaiting he set off back to London. He was pleased to delegate mopping up operations to the Nevilles.

Northumberland historian Cadwallader Bates casts an interesting slant on the movements of the defeated Lancastrian court at this time. He contends that Margaret was unable to flee directly into Scotland as she lacked an official safe conduct through the uncertain and dangerous northern marches. Bates asserts, on dubious authority, that she was besieged in Newcastle by the Yorkists under Edward but that she slipped the net to reach Wark on the Tweed. Here she was again beset by Yorkists under Sir John Conyers and Lord Ogle. Bates further contends that she was saved by a Lancastrian contingent, allowing the Queen finally to seek sanctuary north of the border [15].

The King of Scotland at this time was James III, an eight year old boy whose decisions as King were being governed by a regency council. In an all too familiar situation the council was split into factions – the 'Old' lords were led by Bishop Kennedy of St Andrews and the 'Young' championed the widowed Queen, Marie de Gueldres. Queen Margaret was desperate for allies, so much so that she agreed to trade both Carlisle and Berwick, the twin gatehouses of northern England, in exchange for a Scottish alliance. On 25 April 1461, the keys of Berwick were handed over, but the citizens of Carlisle would have no truck with the Scots and grimly barred their gates, refusing the Queen's summons. A joint Scots and Lancastrian expedition was dispatched to deal with Carlisle, an action the Yorkists perceived dangerous enough for Edward to bring forward the date of his coronation to 28 June 1461. This would mean that the young King would be free to lead a march northwards. In the event this proved unnecessary, as the resourceful John Neville, Lord Montagu raised local forces and saw off the besiegers. Margaret had demonstrated not only the measure of her desperation but also an epic disregard for the sentiment of the very northerners she sought to woo, to whom the Scots were a despised and frequent foe. Berwick upon Tweed was destined to belong to the Scots until 1482 when it was re-taken by Richard of Gloucester, at which point it had changed hands no fewer than fourteen times [16]!

In southern England the spark of rebellion flared briefly in East Anglia and, more seriously, in Wales where the Lancastrian lords still held several major castles. By the autumn the Welsh adherents had been bested in the field and their strongholds systematically reduced; by the end of the year only mighty Harlech still held out.

Feeling themselves relatively secure in Northumberland, the Lancastrian lords Dacre, Roos and Richemont Grey launched a raid into Durham. They advanced their banners as far as Brancepeth with King Henry in their train: perhaps they hoped this show of tattered regality might impress locals, but if so they were swiftly disappointed. Lawrence Booth, the Prince Bishop of Durham, had previously been a staunch Lancastrian but had been converted by the great victory at Towton into an equally enthusiastic Yorkist. Booth mustered the county levies and saw the attackers off, forcing them to return to the relative safety of more distant North Northumberland.

In July 1461, Richard Neville, Earl of Warwick, was appointed warden for both east and west marches, ably assisted by his brother John Neville, Lord Montagu. However, Lancastrian resistance persisted:

> The problem here [the north] was a complicated one, Henry VI and his supporters were sheltered and aided by the Scots, and, to a lesser extent, by the French. The region itself was remote, difficult of access and dominated by the great fortresses [17].

During 1461, the Nevilles continued to mop up in Northumberland until September, by which time Alnwick surrendered and a garrison of one hundred men at arms was installed. In early October, Dunstanburgh capitulated and the terms of the surrender were negotiated by the Lancastrian castellan, Sir Ralph Percy. It might be presumed that the Yorkist triumph was complete, but for as long as the defeated court had a base in Scotland, the border would be troubled.

Edward IV, painfully aware of the narrowness of his own affinity and his fragile grip on the sceptre, was prepared to be accommodating to the Lancastrians in an attempt to strengthen his own position. He decided to allow Sir Ralph Percy to remain in charge at Dunstanburgh, but Percy soon reverted. Another Lancastrian, Sir William Tailboys, emerged from Scotland and swiftly re-captured Alnwick. In the west, Lord Dacre seized Naworth [18]

*The Great Seal of
Edward IV*

Both Edward and his lieutenants therefore decided that a diplomatic move, to treat with the Scots and deprive the Lancastrians of a powerbase in Scotland, was a more sensible move. The Earl of Warwick held preliminary talks with Marie de Gueldres in April 1462, followed by a further meeting in July with the Scottish Council. The Council, already divided, seemed determined to sit on the fence and wait upon events.

The Lancastrians were also attempting diplomacy. Henry Beaufort, 3rd Duke of Somerset, embarked with Lord Hungerford on a begging mission to the French court in March 1462; they returned empty handed. Undeterred, Queen Margaret borrowed £290 from the Scots and sailed for France from Kirkcudbright in April, prepared to trade Calais as she had done Berwick [19].

Naworth Castle, a vital bastion in the West

While Warwick sought an accommodation with Mary in Scotland, his forces in Northumberland resumed the offensive. By July 1462 John Neville, Lord Montagu, had regained Naworth, one of the vital bastions in the west. In the east Alnwick once again fell into Yorkist hands whilst Bamburgh was taken by Sir William Tunstall, another Yorkist.

Alarums and excursions continued with a low intensity level of conflict, typical of the border [20]. 'The support and sympathy of the local population worked against what was regarded as a hostile government and enabled even small forces of active rebels to defy it for months on end' [21].

Despite this defiance, the loss of the defensive chain of border castles and the lack of any material support from France or Scotland did not bode well for the House of Lancaster – but Queen Margaret was persistent. On 25 October she made landfall (Worcester asserts, at Bamburgh) with an expedition led by Pierre de Brézé, a Burgundian Lord who was unswervingly loyal to the Queen's cause. The company comprised some 2,000 French mercenaries and the invaders marched inland to Alnwick. The castle was poorly provisioned and promptly surrendered with Lord Hungerford and de Brézé's son being left in command. Meanwhile, Bamburgh was also re-taken by the Lancastrians – the attack was led by Richard Tunstall. In an ironic twist he took the castle from his brother, the Yorkist Sir William Tunstall. Dunstanburgh also changed hands.

These achievements passed control of the border fortresses back into Queen Margaret's hands once again, but there was no popular upsurge in her favour. Whether she intended simply to re-enforce local anti-Yorkist sentiment or whether she was seeking to open a bridgehead for Scottish intervention, remains unclear [22]. What is certain is that, having secured these three key bastions, she immediately took ship with the bulk of her expeditionary force. She was presumably heading for Scotland to persuade them finally to intervene, but the journey was not straightforward. Although Margaret's ship probably reached Leith safely, many of her ships were wrecked or dispersed by adverse weather in the cold, treacherous wastes of the North Sea; her men were scattered and stores and cash were lost. Some four hundred Frenchmen were stranded on the Northumbrian coast, and unable to enter Bamburgh they fell back towards Holy Island, firing what remained of their boats. The French soon found themselves under determined assault from Yorkists led by Lord Ogle and 'One Maners, a squire'. Falling back and barricading the Priory, the French were soon obliged to seek terms [23].

Warkworth Castle

Though clearly wrong-footed by the Queen, Warwick soon recovered and on 30 October 1462 he marched his forces into Northumberland. On 3 November King Edward followed and by the 16 November he had reached Durham, debilitated by a bout of measles which enfeebled him for the rest of the year [24]. Meanwhile the Earl of Warwick vigorously undertook siege operations against the northern castles. Establishing his forward command post at Warkworth, he entrusted the Duke of Norfolk with responsibility for supply and logistics, through the port of Newcastle. The Earl of Kent was charged with reducing Alnwick. Lord Scales, the Earl of Worcester and Sir Ralph Grey were charged with taking Dunstanburgh. Lords Montagu and Ogle were entrusted to take Bamburgh. This was Warwick at his best, a force of attrition, free from the uncertainties and snap decisions necessary in open field. The Earl rode around his outposts daily and the supply from Newcastle moved smoothly, despite the onset of winter and the desperate state of the roads.

The tactical initiative had swung the other way: John Paston recorded that the Earl of Warwick had mustered some 10,000 soldiers whilst the Lancastrian Henry Beaufort, 3rd Duke of Somerset, had fewer than 300 defenders [25]. Thorough as these siege preparations were, it appeared that the mere show of strength was sufficient to overawe the defenders. There was no bombardment and the great guns never progressed further than the dockside at Newcastle (there was always a reluctance to use gunfire upon the border castles as they were vital for defence in normal circumstances). Even the lighter field pieces were not deployed, which were prepared for use against Scottish forces had they chosen to intervene. Besides, campaigning during a miserable Northumbrian winter had scant appeal:

> Tough, hardy and used to discomfort as they were, medieval soldiers had a deep distaste for winter campaigning ... Henry V had forced his armies to maintain winter sieges in Northern France, but no one had yet attempted them in the even bleaker conditions of Northumbria in December [26].

On Christmas Eve 1462, the Lancastrian Lords negotiated the surrender of both Bamburgh and Dunstanburgh. The terms were the abandonment of their allegiance to Henry VI – if they did so, both Somerset and Sir Ralph Percy were to have their titles and their property restored to them. Both swore fealty to Edward IV. This capitulation may have reflected a loss of morale, because although neither fortress was seriously threatened there appeared little hope of relief once a siege began. Further, it seems that Henry Beaufort, 3rd Duke of Somerset, may well have been resentful of the Frenchman de Brézé being given overall authority over his head. Edward, for his part, was surprisingly pragmatic, when one remembers that the blood of his father, brother, uncle and cousin, stained Somerset's hands [27].

In the meantime the remaining garrison at Alnwick maintained its defiance. They had cause for comfort as the indefatigable de Brézé was leading a Scots relief force. Warwick appears to have been crippled with indecision, a weakness which gripped him in moments of crisis, undoing his careful planning and rigid control of events. He withdrew his forces before Alnwick with such indecent haste that the Scots were led into believing they were being lured into an ambush. This produced a near-farcical dénouement as the Scots speedily withdrew, leaving only a skeleton force. The besiegers then re-occupied the lines they had so recently abandoned [28]. A potentially disastrous situation actually worked to Warwick's advantage as the Lancastrians in Alnwick were left without their Scottish reinforcements! The depleted garrison wasted no time in coming to terms and Warwick appointed Sir John Astley to its command, with Ralph Grey as deputy. Grey considered this a demotion which he bitterly resented, believing that the senior post should have been his. As was so often the case, this personal grudge would bear bitter fruit [29].

By the end of 1462 the position appeared to have returned to that of the summer before Queen Margaret's return – the Yorkists held the border castles once more. This time however, their grip was not as tight; Sir Ralph Percy had sworn allegiance to Edward but at heart was a Lancastrian, and Grey was nursing his resentment. In the spring of 1463 Percy reverted, opening the gates of Bamburgh whilst Grey seized Alnwick by a coup de main:

> And within three or four months after that false knight and traitor, Sir Ralph Percy, by false treason, took the said Sir John Astley prisoner, and delivered him to Queen Margaret, and then delivered the castle to the Lord Hungerford and unto the Frenchmen accompanied with him [30].

Having neatly reversed the position in Northumberland once again, the Lancastrians concentrated their efforts against Norham, the 'Queen of Border Fortresses' belonging to the Prince Bishop of Durham. Frustrated by the loss of Alnwick, Bamburgh and now Dunstanburgh, which Sir Ralph Percy had also gifted back to the Lancastrians, Warwick moved swiftly and relieved Norham castle. His brother Lord Montagu, arriving before the walls, scattered Queen Margaret and her company after a lightning march. So swift and sure was this riposte that both she and King Henry were nearly taken and the Lancastrian garrisons at Norham made no attempt to interfere.

In spite of this success the Earl decided not to besiege the coastal castles (presumably wising to avoid another round of to-ing and fro-ing between Lancastrian and Yorkist possession). He decided instead to put diplomatic pressure on the Scots and thus cut off the Lancastrians' aid at source. Warwick could undoubtedly sense that enthusiasm for the House of Lancaster was waning as the Scots' efforts at Carlisle and Norham had been contemptuously repulsed. With Berwick secure in their hands it seems the Scots had little more to contest. Henry, sensing the mood swing of his hosts, transferred his truncated court either to Alnwick or Bamburgh [31].

In order further to discourage Scottish support for the Lancastrians,

King Edward had obtained a grant of taxation revenues from the English Parliament which he intended to use against them in the field if necessary. Warwick precipitated this offensive action and, with the support of the Archbishop of York, launched a destructive chevauchée into the Lothians [32].

'Save my son; keep him for me; and if God grant his restoration, be sure that he will well reward a service such as never yet hath fallen to the lot of a man like thee to perform'

The words of
Queen Margaret in
Cadwallader Bates' History

The historian Cadwallader Bates places Queen Margaret, her son and de Brézé in the environs of Hexham on 3 April 1463. He also reports a Lancastrian force (augmented by French mercenaries and Scots) advancing from the direction of the town of Hexham to take up 'Rel' or Ryal on the banks of Devil's Water, a small local river. Here they were confronted by John Neville, Lord Montagu, and the Franco-Scots were dispersed. The Queen also was forced to take to her heels in the rout with only her son and a single squire! Bates describes how she sought refuge in nearby Dipton Wood, losing her sole protector in the flight. Again according to Bates, she was then accosted by a notorious local outlaw whom she won over with a display of regal courage, and with this new ally she hid out in a forest cave before making good her escape [33]. Popular legend asserts that the cave in question is that which is located below the crags on

106

the left bank of the West Dipton Burn, some three miles west of Linnels Bridge, and now dubbed 'The Queen's Cave'. This is almost certainly a later accretion, which the historian has polished to a fine gloss.

Norham Castle
'The Queen of Border Fortresses'
guarded a ford over the Tweed

It is not, of course, entirely impossible that this or a similar incident occurred by Norham [34]. Tempting as it may be to conjecture a skirmish in 1463, none of the chronicles corroborates it. We know that Margaret and de Brézé were both present at the siege of Norham and that their forces were surprised and scattered by Montagu. Bates also mentions, as a separate instance, that King Henry VI and his son Edward subsisted for five days in another cave, with 'only a single herring between them'. The facts of the two alleged incidents appear remarkably similar and, if such a fine tale did occur, then surely it must have been at Norham. Neither Margaret nor de Brézé was present at the Battle of Hexham, fought the following year [35].

After the débâcle at Norham, Queen Margaret, fearful for her son, took ship for Flanders, accompanied by de Brézé, where she proposed to solicit aid from Duke Philip 'the Good' of Burgundy. The wily Burgundian and his son, the Count of Charolais (known later as Philip 'the Bold'), showed signs of encouragement. Charles VII also wrote reassuringly to Henry, now safely within Bamburgh's stout walls. No practical assistance, however, was forthcoming.

Gregory [36] asserts that the Lancastrians then sailed immediately from Sluys in France and were pursued for the whole journey back – almost to the walls of Bamburgh! Margaret and her shrunken contingent included Exeter, Fortescue and the remaining Frenchmen. Together, they filled four 'balynggarys' (ballingers): large, sleek, double ended and oared galleys, frequently deployed against pirates in the Channel. Gregory recounts that a French drummer boy refused to embark and waited calmly on the shore. This disenchanted youth demanded vociferously a place in Warwick's retinue and the Earl acquiesced, the renegade doing good service for a number of years [37].

In Bamburgh, King Henry was molested neither by Warwick nor his brother Montagu and maintained a façade of lordship over his Lilliputian domain. In December 1463 he issued letters of protection to William Burgh, Constable of Prudhoe, seeking to consolidate the Lancastrian influence in Tynedale, where sentiment for the cause remained viable. Early in the New Year Henry also issued a charter to the burgesses of Edinburgh. A French ambassador, Pierre Cousinot, attended this shadow court and the King used him as a messenger to contact his wife in Burgundy. Henry proposed a strategy comprising a tripartite alliance between himself as titular King of England, the Count of Charolais and the Duke of Brittany.

He pleaded with the great lords of France to work against any understanding that might be brokered between Edward IV and Louis XI (who succeeded to the French throne on the death of Charles VII). He begged aid from the Burgundians and pleaded for aid and ordnance from René of Anjou, his father-in-law. He entreated the Bretons to exploit unrest in Wales and to join with the Earl of Pembroke. All of these pleas were persuasive, but Henry's main difficulty was lack of funds and all of his plans included a request for cash. Deprived of parliamentary grants, destitute of lands and treasure and with no fiscal base to fund aggressive action, his faction had no real leadership. In 1464 the prospects for the Lancastrians seemed utterly bleak and yet, in the spring of that year, the rogue card, Henry Beaufort, 3rd Duke of Somerset, reverted to the House of Lancaster. This reversion would spark the final, dramatic episodes of the War in the North.

Notes:

[1] *Calendar of State Papers and Manuscripts existing in the Archives and Collections of Milan* ed. and transl. Hinds A B pp.74-77

[2] Pollard A J, *'Characteristics of the Fifteenth Century North'* in 'Government Religion and Society in Northern England 1000-1700' ed. Appleby C & Dalton P England 1977 p.131

[3] Hepple L W, *'A History of Northumberland and Newcastle upon Tyne'* London 1976 pp.14-15

[4] Ibid. p.15

[5] Ibid. p.39

[6] Lomas R, *'County of Conflict'* Edinburgh 1996 pp. 51-52

[7] Ibid. p.94

[8] Ibid. p.90

[9] Ibid. p.55

[10] Pevsner N and Richmond I *'The Buildings of England: Northumberland'* 2nd Edition London 1992 pp. 135-136

[11] Long B, *'The Castles of Northumberland'* p. 67 William the Lion had been defeated in a lightening attack before the walls of Alnwick in 1174 and captured.

[12] Pevsner and Richmond op. cit. pp. 155-156

[13] Ibid. pp.258-259

[14] Charlesworth D, *'Northumberland in the Early years of Edward IV'* in Archaeologia Aeliana 4th Series 1953 p.70

[15] Bates C J, *'History of Northumberland'* London 1895 p.195

[16] Lomas op. cit. pp.45-50

[17] Ross C, *'Wars of the Roses'* London 1976 p.56

[18] Gillingham J, *'The Wars of the Roses'* 1981 pp. 140-141

[19] *Scottish Exchequer Rolls* vii Ramsay ii p.290

[20] Gillingham op. cit. p.141

[21] Ross op. cit. p.60

[22] Worcester, *'Annales'* p.480

[23] *NCH* vol I p.48

[24] Worcester, *'Annales'* p.480

[25] *Paston Letters* no. 464

[26] Ross op. cit. pp.62-63

[27] *Gregory's Chronicle* p.219

[28] Ibid. p.219

[29] Ibid. p.220

[30] Ibid. p.221

[31] *'The year Book de Termino Paschae 4 Edward IV'* in Priory of Hexham, Surtes Society p. cviii gives Alnwick as the location but NCH vol 1 p.46 claims Bamburgh – the latter seems more likely being on the coast and closer to Scotland.

[32] Ross op. cit. p.65

[33] Bates op. cit. pp.198-199. Bates gives Chastellain as his authority, who claims he heard the story from the Queen herself, though this version is somewhat circumstantial, see Chastellain G 'Chroniques des derniers Ducs de Bourgoyne' in Pantheon Litteraire iv pp.230-232

[34] Tomlinson W W, *'Comprehensive Guide to Northumberland'* Newcastle upon Tyne 1863 pp.112-113

[34] Bates op. cit. p.199

[35] *Gregory's Chronicle* p.222

[36] Ibid. p.222

[37] *NCH* 1 p.46

PART SEVEN

HEDGELEY MOOR AND HEXHAM

Henry Beaufort, his brother in law Sir Henry Lewis and Sir Nicholas Latimer had all been attainted in 1461 when they were in Dunstanburgh, and the fortress finally surrendered on 27 December 1462. In the circumstances they were treated with extraordinary leniency. On 17 March 1463 Sir Ralph Percy – who had also been granted leniency – received a commission to accept the submission of the other rebels. This act reflected an element of *realpolitik*: Percy was a name that still carried great weight in Northumberland. If King Edward could secure the Percy allegiance he would effectively kick away the greatest Lancastrian prop in the north, so the potential gain was worth the risk.

It is a strange occurrence that Henry Beaufort surrendered and defected to the Yorkist camp, as he probably could have escaped with most of the garrison and been granted safe conduct until he reached Scotland. Beaufort probably knew, however, that the Earl of Warwick would go to great lengths to pursue him. As a commander-in-chief of the Lancastrian faction, Beaufort would always be a threat when at large. With this knowledge in mind it seems that the former Duke had already approached Warwick some months before to explore terms.

Battle of Towton, 29 March 1461

Henry Percy, 3rd Earl of Northumberland, was one of the of thousands killed on this day

Henry Beaufort fared well as a Yorkist. He appears to have served with some distinction against his former Lancastrian associates and he possessed the charisma and fortitude of the Beauforts. King Edward made much of him and the former enemies hunted together and indeed Beaufort even enjoyed the signal honour of acting as a knight of the bedchamber, a position of special trust since it involved protecting the king as he slept. He received cash subsidies and the hefty annuity of a thousand marks. Tournaments were mounted in his honour and the King intervened personally to save him from certain death at the hands of an unruly mob in Northampton [1]. On 10 March 1463, his attainder was reversed and Henry Beaufort became Duke of Somerset once more.

And yet, by December 1463, Henry Beaufort and Ralph Percy had both reverted to the House of Lancaster. Hicks has asserted, probably correctly, that this change of heart was due neither to stupidity nor to an unwillingness to accept reality; Somerset was no fool and he must have known that King Henry's chance of success was not good. What seems to have occurred was a crisis of conscience. The oath he had given to Henry VI was too compelling to ignore and integrity triumphed over expediency. The cause may have been hopeless, but for Somerset it seems that honour outweighed the odds [2], as it did with Ralph Percy. Possibly both Percy and Somerset regarded their earlier compromises as being nothing more than a necessary ruse to gain time until circumstances changed for the better.

Latimer and Lewis also reverted to the House of Lancaster between 1469 and 1471, as did Sir Henry Bellingham and Sir Humphrey Neville. Some commentators, particularly Ross, regard Edward's policy of 'hearts and minds' as naïve and culpable, a political blunder [3]. This may be too harsh on Edward: he had, after all, won the crown by the sword and his affinity amongst the magnates was dangerously narrow. To survive and establish a stable regime he did need to broaden his platform of support by winning over former opponents. Simply killing them was not an effective policy – as shown following St Albans in 1455 with the deaths of the elder Henry Percy and Edmund Beaufort. The blood spilled on the streets of St Albans had pooled into a legacy of hate and resentment that led, ultimately, to the carnage of Towton. The effects of this titanic fight should not be underestimated: the Yorkists had won, but only by a whisker, and no Prince would consider repeating such an epic campaign so soon – the drain on blood and treasure would be too great. Edward had judged that suborning (or bribing) his former enemies not only brought new friends but demoralised the remaining diehards. By the close of 1462, he would have been justified in thinking that his enemies' swords were irrevocably made into ploughshares and the flames of resistance guttered out [4].

Edward's contemporaries certainly took a harsher view. Gregory, no friend to Somerset, was unimpressed by Edward's magnanimity. He observed that:

> 'the savynge of hys lyffe at that tyme cuasyd mony mannys dethys son aftyr, as ye shalle heyre' [5].

Hicks views Percy's defection as more serious than that of Somerset, because of the power of his name in Northumberland, notwithstanding the fact that King Edward still held Somerset's brother and Percy's nephew as hostages [6]. Edward's policy of conciliation had been at best a gamble, and one which, in these significant instances, clearly failed [7]. At the time it seemed a risk worth taking if the prize was a lasting peace, but this was not achieved and the Lancastrian cause in the North enjoyed one final, brief revival in the spring of 1464 [8]. Sporadic unrest erupted throughout the realm early in the year. In fifteen counties, from Kent to Cornwall and as far north as Leicestershire, the disruption was sufficiently serious for the King to delay the state opening of Parliament. There is evidence from the contemporary record that Somerset may have mistakenly perceived that King Henry had received fresh impetus and supplies:

'herynge y King Henry was comynge into the lande with a newe strength' [9].

It is uncertain where these fresh troops were coming from and how they were to be paid; perhaps there was a hope the French might intervene, or even the Scots. Somerset would have been under no illusion as to his fate should he fail; the clemency he had enjoyed was exceptional and it would not be extended a second time. He established his reversion by attempting to seize Newcastle which would have been a considerable prize, being the Yorkists' forward supply base. A number of his affinity began to infiltrate the garrison but the attempt did not succeed because Lord Scrope, with some of the King's household knights, frustrated the scheme. The rebel Duke was very nearly taken at Durham where he was obliged to flee from his lodgings dressed only in his nightshirt! Gregory reports that a number of his retainers were captured, together with their master's 'caskette and hys harneys [helmet and armour]' [10]. Any others who were caught attempting to escape from Newcastle suffered summary execution.

There are some further doubts even today as to where the fugitive King Henry was based at this time. In the 'Year Book' it claims that he was based at Alnwick, though this may be incorrect because the same source claims that Queen Margaret and de Brézé were with him, when we can be certain they were actually both in Flanders [11]. NCH, however, places his diminished court at lordly Bamburgh and this seems more credible: Alnwick was nearer the Yorkists in Newcastle and Bamburgh had access to the sea [12].

Somerset may have proceeded straight to Henry's court or possibly made for Tynedale, where the castles of Prudhoe, Bywell and Langley remained staunchly Lancastrian. At some point in February or March, Somerset was joined by his former comrades Ralph Percy and Sir Humphrey Neville of Brancepeth, with their retainers. With the Duke's return to the Lancastrian fold a new sense of purpose and urgency had infused the faltering cause.

And urgency there was, for the Scots were showing willingness to treat with Warwick and provide safe passage for his brother, Lord Monatgu, through the frontier area in order to have talks with a team of Scottish peace negotiators. These talks were scheduled to take place in Newcastle on 6 March 1464, but the increasing tempo of alarums delayed the meeting. The venue shifted southward to calmer pastures and the meeting was scheduled for 20 April. On 27 March, Edward announced his intention to travel North in order to organise a suitable escort for the Scottish delegation who were waiting at Norham for proceedings to begin [13].

A successful meeting between Monatgu and the Scots would be fatal to Lancastrian hopes and so Somerset, staking everything, dispatched a commanded body of foot: 'four score spears and bows too' [14], under Sir Humphrey Neville of Brancepeth, to lay an ambush 'a little from Newcastle in a wood' [15]. Forewarned by scouts or spies, Montagu easily avoided this trap and chose a safer route into the city where he was reinforced by 'a great fellowship' [16]. He then set out to march northwards to the border.

Somerset's best chance now lay in forcing a decisive encounter, causing a defeat in the field. This would leave the Scots immured, isolated in Norham where the Yorkists could not reach them, at the same time demonstrating that the Lancastrians still had teeth. By mustering every spear he could find and by stripping his handful of garrisons the Duke might, as Gregory suggests, have been able to muster 5,000 men [17]. This seems a very generous estimate, even if he could count upon his own affinity, along with those of Ralph Percy, Humphrey Neville, Bellingham, Lords Hungerford and Roos and the turncoat Grey. We have no note of the force Montagu was leading north but it would certainly have been the equal of anything his enemies could deploy.

As the Yorkists marched north from Morpeth, the Lancastrians sallied from Alnwick, both sides probing with a screen of light horse or 'prickers'. Such work was meat and drink to the borderers, bred to war. Nine miles west of Alnwick, Somerset drew up in battle order, blocking the way northwards to Norham where the Scots were waiting. Though the chronicles provide only scant details of the battle which ensued, a careful perambulation of the ground indicates that the fight (the Battle of Hedgeley Moor) took place on the shelf of rising ground just north of where Percy's Cross now

Hedgeley Moor

On this terrain the hopes of the Lancastrrian cause in the north floundered

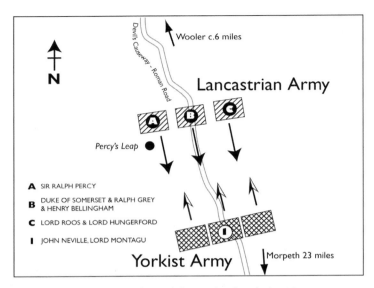

The opening phase of the Battle of Hedgeley Moor

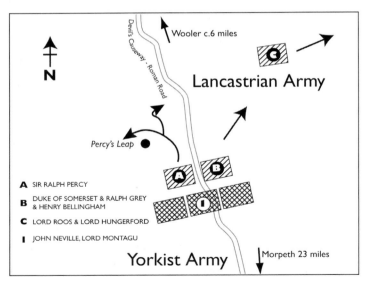

The closing phase of the Battle of Hedgeley Moor

stands. This is the area between a wood known as Percy's Strip Wood and the monument, 'Percy's Leap'.

Here the ground is roughly level, slightly undulating and rising toward the northern flank. In the spring of 1464 the land was not under the plough, but was an expanse of open moor, largely devoid of trees. With the Lancastrians facing south, in front of Percy's leap, it is most likely that the Yorkists carried out their initial deployment on the line of the present woodland.

As they approached from the south, the main body of the Yorkists would have had no opportunity to view the strength of their enemy until they ascended the slight rise. Haigh [18] shows the Yorkists drawn up somewhat to the south of this position and indicates that the Lancastrians advanced to contact over open ground. This is unlikely because Yorkist morale was high and Montagu may have enjoyed greater strength; he was by nature a confident and aggressive commander. This is, however, conjectural as the chronicles remain frustratingly silent as to these initial dispositions and the numbers certainly cannot be assessed with any degree of confidence [19]. Somerset, although energetic, may have been similar to Warwick in that he was indecisive at key moments: his failure to reinforce Clifford during the skirmish at Dintingdale in 1461 stands as a clear example [20].

It may be that the fight began with the customary duel of arrows and that Yorkist supremacy was swiftly asserted. Before ever striking a blow the whole of the Lancastrian left or rearward division, commanded by Hungerford and Roos, dissolved in total rout. This left the centre under Somerset, Bellingham and Grey, together with the right or vaward, under Percy, horribly exposed. Montagu ordered the advance to contact [21]. The mêlée, a short, savage and largely one-sided encounter, almost certainly

Boulders, thirty feet apart, at Percy's Leap
may mark the death throes
of Ralph Percy's horse

occurred in the vicinity of Percy's Leap. The Lancastrian centre soon joined their fellows in flight, Somerset and his officers swept along also. By this time Sir Ralph Percy was surrounded by the enemy, accompanied only by his closest retainers; wounded but still on horseback. Slashing desperately at his attackers, he struggled bravely to redeem his earlier disloyalty. It is related that eventually his horse was hit by arrows, making a valiant leap as it died – the distance marked even today by two boulders at the site – and his master fell onto the waiting blades of his foes. An intriguing legend lingers over his last moments – 'I have saved the bird in my bosom,' he is said to have uttered, as his mount stumbled the dozen yards between two low outcrops. What he meant by this enigmatic phrase remains uncertain: perhaps he referred to his true loyalty to Henry VI – ironic then, from a man who had changed sides with such facility [22]. Montagu's victory was complete, but apart from Percy and those retainers around him, most of the defeated escaped unscathed. Despite their humiliation on the field, the Lancastrians' survival meant that Somerset was able to rally many of them in retreat, to regroup in Tynedale.

Percy's Cross at Hedgeley Moor reputedly marks the site of Ralph Percy's gallant last stand

Montagu was then able to continue to Norham to meet up with the Scottish peace envoys. With the Scots now in negotiations, and the French also in talks at St Omer (which had begun the previous autumn), the Lancastrians' diplomatic isolation was all but complete. As Northumberland was no longer viable as a bridgehead there was little incentive for Somerset to disperse his forces in isolated garrisons; simply holding ground was pointless. With the Scots set to change horses, bargaining chips like Berwick and Norham had no further currency [23].

Henry's prospects appeared brighter in the west, for in March there were some fresh disturbances in Lancashire and Cheshire. Resistance flared briefly in Skipton in Craven, seat of the Cliffords, who, with their local affinity, had bled so liberally for Lancaster. None of these alarums developed into a serious threat [24], but King Edward felt insecure enough to send out commissions of array to the Midlands and Yorkshire (which allowed him to call up local militia to fight for him); no writs were issued in Northumberland, Cumberland, Westmorland, Lancashire or Cheshire [25].

Both sides were short of cash. Edward had been granted subsidies to prosecute the war in the North; Norham had been relieved, but beyond that nothing much had been achieved in the field except Montagu's notable success at Hedgeley Moor. Little had been directly attempted against the Scots, and a further grant from Parliament had been gobbled up by existing commitments, particularly the garrison at Calais [26].

The Yorkist administration was surviving on loans and was substantially in debt; raising taxes built resentment in all quarters, and this umbrage was exacerbated when there was no tangible gain. So vociferous was the disaffection that in the November of the previous year (1463) the King had felt constrained to remit some £6,000 of the subsidy granted in the summer [27].

Somerset was under even greater pressure; with no taxation revenue, no grants and no other subsidies he was obliged to beg, borrow and steal. Even when monies *could* be scraped together, a proportion would disappear through defalcation (fraud and misappropriation). Tellingly, when Lord Tailboys was captured hiding in a coal pit after the Battle of Hexham, he was loaded with pilfered funds:

> 'He hadde moch money with hym, both golde and sylvyr, that shulde hav gon unto King Harry; and yf it had come to Harry, lat kynge of Ingelonde, hyt wolde have causyd moche sore sorowe, for he had ordynyd harneys and ordenance i-nowe, but the men wolde not go one fote with hym tylle they had mony' [28].

Henry now appears to have moved his lodgings to Bywell Castle near Corbridge, in Tynedale; he was in residence by the latter part of April 1464. Bywell was not a significant castle and possessed no strategic value: it was the gatehouse tower of an unfinished castle built in 1430 by Ralph Neville, Earl of Westmorland, whose family had held the barony from the time of Edward III. After the Battle of Hexham the victors found evidence there of a hurried departure: the King's helmet or 'bycoket' (a coroneted cap),

The Gatehouse of Bywell Castle, part of Ralph Neville's unfinished fortifications

'richly garnysshed wt ij crownys, and his followers trapped wt blew velvet' [29].

Both Tynedale and Redesdale were administered as 'Liberties' – franchises where the crown sub-contracted the business of local government to franchisees, which led to a fair measure of autonomy. The Lancastrians still had a foothold in Tynedale, holding Hexham, Prudhoe and possibly other centres [32].

The Liberty of Tynedale covered a wide sweep of ground, some 200,000 acres in all, encompassing the valleys of the North and South Tyne with the Allen; in the 13th Century it had been a fief of the Scottish crown. Hexham 'shire' was an area of some 80,000 acres, a fertile, alluvial tract of the North Tyne, rising to the rough moorlands around Allendale [33]. How much local support the Lancastrian cause enjoyed is questionable – the northern lords, Percy, Dacre and Clifford, had bled freely and their affinities were now thinned and leaderless. There was a rumour that their number might have been bolstered by 'a great power out of Scotlade' [30], but these were more likely to have been riders from Liddesdale and Teviotdale, drawn by the scent of booty. Much had changed since the halcyon days of 1459-1460 when Queen Margaret had been able to offer free quarter and plunder as incentives. By 1464 her cause had been depleted by the catastrophe of Towton and by three further years of attrition [34].

As mentioned above, there is no firm indication of how long King Henry remained at Bywell. Although some sources relate that he fled after the Battle of Hexham, he probably left before the battle took place – Somerset would have been a fool to leave the king so exposed. We know that by the end of the first week in May, Montagu returned to Newcastle from York, having delivered the Scots envoys, being aware, probably through espionage, that there was Lancastrian activity in Tynedale. On this occasion he was not distracted by diplomatic activity with the Scots and could concentrate his considerable abilities toward achieving a decisive outcome. Thus:

> 'on xiii of May, my lorde Mountague toke his jornaye toward Hexham from Newcastelle' [35].

Advancing with his forces strung along the north bank of the Tyne, Hexham was the immediate tactical objective, his intention being to eliminate the Lancastrian presence once and for all. Somerset would have been well aware of this and though some Tudor chroniclers assert that King Henry was present on the field, Gregory suggests that he had fled north to Scotland. In fact, Henry probably made for the west, to Lancashire – Scotland no longer being safe for him. It is believed that Montagu crossed the Tyne either at Bywell or Corbridge, adding weight to the argument that Henry had already left the area – had he remained he might easily have been taken prisoner. Only the line of the Devil's Water now stood between Montagu and the Lancastrian base of Hexham [36]. Devil's Water is a small river which carries romantic overtones from the later Jacobite era; it follows a meandering course from the high ground of the Shire towards the Tyne. From Hexham the ground shelves markedly toward a crossing at Linnels Bridge, some two miles from the town; on the south of the river the land rises steeply in the direction of Slaley.

The traditional and long accepted site for the battle of Hexham lies south of the present B6306, on low ground (the 'Hexham Levels') by the banks of the stream, as featured on the OS 1:25000 map. However, in spite of the long standing acceptance of this location, the evidence is neither compelling nor uncontentious.

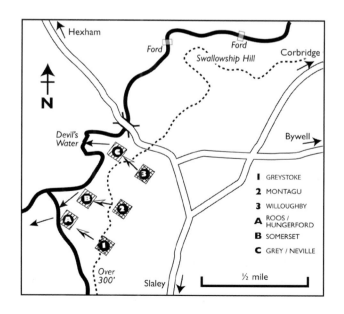

The traditional site of the Battle of Hexham

The best contemporary source, the Year Book describes the actual field as *un lieu appelle Livels sur le ewe Devyls* [37]. Worcester says that it took place on a hill one mile from Hexham, suggesting unequivocally rising ground [38]. The Year Book, which also states that the fight occurred on 15 May, merely points to Linnels as the general area. Ramsay, who had visited the location or talked to someone who had, observes tellingly that '[the site] is a nice, sheltered camping ground … but a very bad battlefield' [39]. In accord with Ramsay, Charlesworth observes that the low ground is a most unsuitable site [40].

It appears clear from a perambulation of the area that the traditional understanding of the location of the battle is indeed badly flawed: to the rear it is hemmed by the water and to the front by steeply rising ground. This impedes visibility, inhibits manoeuvre and makes a gift of the heights above to the attacker. Later writers accepted this position as the battleground [41] without re-examining the topography and considering the implications. Charlesworth argues cogently that while Somerset may have camped on the Levels, he did not deploy for battle there. Rather, on the morning of 15 May, he drew his forces up on the higher ground along the crest of Swallowship Hill. Had he not done so, Montagu could have outflanked him and gained Hexham from the ford over the Devil's Water directly below the hill. The chroniclers do not really give us any assistance here [42]; we are in the area of 'inherent military probability' as advanced by Colonel Burne, one of the pioneers of modern military history.

If the Lancastrian defenders occupied the rise of Swallowship Hill they could not be outflanked, as the crest of the hill commands a good view of all of the viable crossings over the river. As the ground drops quite sharply toward Devil's Water, this would have forced the Yorkist troops to attack the centre of Somerset's army, the line of his men curving to match the

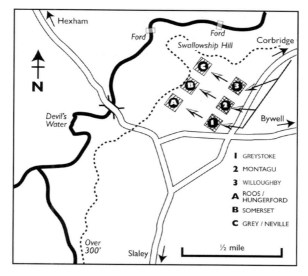

Opening phase of the Battle of Hexham

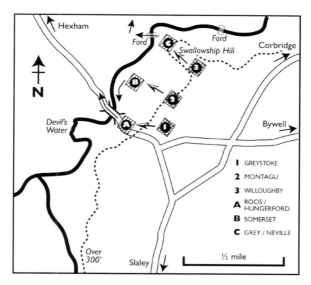

Final phase of the Battle of Hexham

contours of the landscape. He may have taken the centre with Grey and Neville commanding on the left, Hungerford and Roos on the right.

Swallowship Hill where the forces under Montagu and Somerset clashed
Duke's House can be seen on the horizon

Charlesworth asserts that the Lancastrians dominated all of the local crossing points of the river: the ford which lay below, Earl's Bridge to the north, Linnels Bridge (then probably also a ford) and the more southerly ford by Newbiggin. This is conjecture, but the nature of the ground clearly favours Charlesworth's theory. This, then, was likely to be the deployment which confronted Lord Montagu. He probably fielded more troops and they would have had higher morale, since Hedgeley had been a relatively easy victory. Both of his flank commanders, Lords Greystoke and Willoughby, were former Lancastrians.

Whether the fight began with a duel of arrows is not recorded. The Yorkists may well have advanced rapidly to contact and the mêlée was

A 1900s photograph by J P Gibson showing the steep banks of Devils Water below Swallowship Hill

both sharp and short. Hungerford and Roos, on the Lancastrian right, were again the first to give ground, and the line dissolved. Somerset may have tried to cling to the crest and rally, but he was swept away in the confusion and panic. The ford was soon choked with fleeing men, the brief fight over; only the business of pursuit remained [43].

Casualties in the combat were almost certainly very light since the chroniclers do not mention any knights killed on the field. More gentle blood by far was spilt by the executioners in the spree of slaughter which followed. Worcester asserts, but it is difficult to credit, that Montagu fielded 10,000 men against Somerset's 500 [44] but no commander would accept battle against such odds; it's more likely that the Duke of Somerset only had 500 *of his household men*, these being but a proportion of his whole force.

Conversely, Warkworth argues that the Lancastrians had 'gathered a great people in the north country' and that the Yorkists were outnumbered, having no more than 4,000 men [45]. Looking at the ground, the location on Swallowship Hill covers a front of around 1,000 yards. Allowing one man per yard and a gap between divisions, a force of at least 4,000 would be needed to give substance to the deployment. For his part, Montagu would surely have been less enthusiastic to engage had not his army been equal to – or greater than – that of his opponent.

Montagu was not encumbered by the distractions that had attended Hedgeley Moor, and was fully able to harry the fleeing Lancastrians. Somerset, Hungerford and Roos were all taken, captured 'in a wood faste by' [46], although it is said by some that the wounded Somerset was captured having been carried to a nearby cottage, since replaced by a gothic mansion named Duke's House in memory of this event. Somerset could not reasonably have expected any further clemency. Montagu, like his brother Warwick, was not interested in reconciliation; it was now time for retribution. We are obliged to rely upon Gregory for the list of those who were executed in the immediate aftermath of the rout; of these Somerset was by far the most distinguished. The remainder were Edmund Fysche, Edmond Fitzhugh, Miles Bradshawe, Wate (Walter) Hunt and the likely reiver 'Black Jakys [Jack or John], who were of considerably lower standing.

Henry Beaufort, Duke of Somerset, son of a father who had coughed up his lifeblood on the streets of St Albans nearly a decade earlier, could have had no doubts as to his fate. He had taken King Edward's hand in friendship and had then spat in the face of the man who had offered him clemency and power. His campaign of 1464 had the aspect of a desperate gambler's final throw, a wager that had cost many men their lives and would now claim his. Some accounts suggest that the Battle of Hexham occurred early in the day (15 May) and that Somerset was executed later that day in Hexham. However, Gregory, our principle source, has it on the following day. Given that (although a turncoat) Somerset was a peer descended from John of Gaunt, it does seem more likely that time would be needed for his arraignment, trial and sentence, even if there was no doubt of the outcome. We have no record of any final speeches, or of

1900s photograph by J P Gibson, of Hexham Goal,
where Somerset probably spent the time before his execution

whether the Duke met his death with equanimity, but we may assume that he did – faint-heartedness was not a family characteristic.

Hexham market-place was then, as now, an area defined on the west by the bulk of the Abbey and, on the east, by the Moot Hall and Gaol. Tall and narrow timber-framed houses, a riot of structures perched like ungainly storks, crowded the north and south. We can surmise, and it is nothing more, that the condemned men spent their final night crammed into the Gaol, and that they had been swiftly condemned by a semblance of a trial. Stripped of arms and harness they would be brought out on a warm spring morning, perhaps the sort where the light catches the fresh green of the sprouting leaves and blue skies lift the spirits, a poor sort of day for the grim business of the headsman's axe. It is likely that a rough dais had been constructed and an expectant crowd would already have gathered. Would Somerset be killed first or last? Any decent showman

Beheading of Edmund Beaufort at Tewkesbury in 1471, a similar fate had befallen his brother, Henry Beaufort, in Hexham 1464

would save him, the main attraction, to be the last to die.

Thus Henry Beaufort, Third Duke of Somerset, in whose veins was the blood of kings, would be led to the scaffold. His hands would be bound after he had been stripped of his doublet and a priest would be in attendance as he was made to kneel. A sombre roll of drums would silence the crowd as the headsman prepared to do his work. It was customary for the victim to tip the executioner to avoid a botched job and to offer

Hexham Abbey
Somewhere in its precincts is the burial site of the Duke of Somerset.

Plaque commemorating the execution of the Duke of Somerset in the market place at Hexham

forgiveness for the sin to be committed. He would kneel forward over the block, neck exposed and extended to facilitate a clean stroke.

As a Peer he would be permitted to extend an arm to dictate the time that the blade should fall. As his arm fell, the axe would follow, cleaving down in a fearful arc of honed precision, the razor-edged blade would lop off the head in a single, final stroke. The severed head would tumble onto the dais or into a basket, and blood would splash any spectator who had edged too close.

This was but the beginning, the curtain-raiser to a full and thorough purge. A rash of executions ensued – at Newcastle on 17 May: Lords Hungerford and Roos, Sir Thomas Fyndorne, Barnarde de la Mare and Nicholas Massam. The following day at Middleham: Sir Philip Wentworth, William Penyngton, the ward of Topcliff, Olyver Wentworthe, William Spyller, John Senyer and Thomas Haute. On 26 May at York: Sir Thomas Hoosy, Thomas Gosse, Robert Myrfyn, John Butler, Robert Wattys (formerly porter to Henry VI), Thomas Fenwyke, Robert Cockefelde, William Bryce, Wylliam Dawson, John Chapman, John Edyrbeke, Rycharde Taverner, John Russelle and Robert Conqueror. The *Short English Chronicle* agrees with Gregory in relation to those killed both at Hexham and Newcastle but adds to the list of those who subsequently died at York Sir Thomas Hull and Thomas Hegge.

The house of Lancaster in the north was ruined, Somerset and the rebel lords hunted out, their retainers scattered. Humphrey Neville managed to escape – he had previously escaped from the Tower and possessed a genius for survival – with Sir Ralph Grey and the remnant, regaining Bamburgh, where the reduced garrison maintained a show of defiance.

The embezzling Lord Tailboys was netted and his hoard provided a handy bonus for Montagu's soldiery:

> '.. the sum of 3,000 mark. And the lord's meinie of Montagu were sore hurt and sick, and many of him men were slain before in the great journeys, but this money was departed among them, and was a very wholesome salve for them' [49].

Tailboys was executed at Newcastle on 20 July, the last of the crop of prisoners to face the axe.

Barely two weeks after the Battle of Hexham, John Neville, Lord Montagu, in the presence of both of his brothers, was elevated to the Earldom of Northumberland by the King at York – this was the zenith of the Nevilles' power. While he was in his northern capital (York) Edward ratified the treaty with the Scots, concluded on 11 June, which secured a truce which lasted for fifteen years. Warwick, as the King's lieutenant, was charged once again with the recovery of the three border fortresses.

CR

A Medieval siege gun
similar to ones used in the siege of
Bamburgh Castle

To assist in these operations Edward assembled a formidable siege train, 'the great ordnance of England', the bombards ''Edward', 'Dijon', 'London', 'Newcastle' and 'Richard Bombartel' [50]. The sight of these great guns was enough to overawe the defenders at Alnwick, who capitulated on the 23 June, followed by those at Dunstanburgh the next day.

Bates maintains that Dunstanburgh was stormed and that the governor John Gosse, of Somerset's affinity, was taken and sent southwards to York to face execution [51].

The ruins of
Dunstanburgh Castle
whose defenders
surrendered without a
fight

Bates continues by asserting that Warwick maintained the feast of St John the Baptist at Dunstanburgh while Henry VI was still within the walls of Bamburgh. He further claims that Henry made good his escape with the aid of Sir Henry Bellingham. NCH concurs and suggests that King Henry VI still had a ragged household consisting of Sir Thomas Philip, William Learmouth, Thomas Elwyk of Bamburgh, John Retford of Lincolnshire (described as gentlemen), together with John Purcas of London, a yeoman, Philip Castelle of Pembroke, Archibald and Gilbert Ridley from Langley, Gawen Lampleugh of Warkworth, also a gentleman, John Whynfell of Naworth, yeoman and Alexander Bellingham from Burneside in Westmorland [52].

This is most certainly inaccurate; none of those mentioned appears to have fought at Hexham and, if he did, there is no evidence that he definitely evaded capture. It is more likely that these individuals were in the King's service before the débacle on Devil's Water and fled westwards at the same time. Bates, with the NCH, suggests that Sir Ralph Grey also escaped back to Bamburgh *before* the Battle of Hexham, rather than after [53]. Once again this seems unconvincing: Grey and his retainers would be needed on the field and Bamburgh was very much a last resort for a defeated captain who was all too aware that his duplicity excluded him from amnesty.

Though perhaps the greatest of the Northumbrian fortresses, Bamburgh was not built to withstand cannon and the deployment of the royal train before its massive walls gave ample notice of deadly intent. The Earl of Warwick dispatched his own and the King's heralds formally to demand the surrender of the garrison. They offered quarter to the commons, but both Grey and Neville were excluded from any terms, being 'out of the King's grace without any redemption' [54].

Grey, with nothing to lose, breathed defiance; he was clearly determined to live or die in the castle. The heralds responded with a stern rejoinder and one can hear the stentorian voice of the Earl of Warwick resonating through the chronicler's account:

> 'The King, our most dread sovereign lord, specially desires to have this jewel whole and unbroken by artillery, particularly because it stands so close to his ancient enemies the Scots, and if you are the cause that great guns have to be fired against its walls, then it will cost you your head, and for every shot that has to be fired another head down to the humblest person within the place' [55].

Thus began the only siege bombardment of the Wars. The bombards 'Newcastle' and 'London' were dragged into place and the elevation fixed. They were then loaded and the firing began, the crash of the reports echoing as at the crack of doom. A great sulphurous cloud of filthy smoke drifted over the embattled ramparts as whole sections of masonry were

The imposing bastion of Bamburgh Castle
whose walls were damaged by cannon fire in 1464

137

blasted by roundshot and crashed into the sea [56]. It was, however, the lighter gun 'Dijon' firing several rounds through the chamber that had the most effect: Grey had established his HQ in the eastern gatehouse and it was here that he was injured, rendered insensible when one of the besiegers' rounds brought down part of the roof [57]

Humphrey Neville of Brancepeth (a Lancastrian Neville), ever the survivor, seized the moment to seek terms, securing clemency for the garrison and, cleverly, for himself. The dazed Sir Ralph was tied to his horse and escorted unwillingly as far as Doncaster to be tried by Sir John Tiptoft, Earl of Worcester and Constable of England. One of the indictments lodged against him was that he 'had withstood and made fences against the king's majesty, and his lieutenant, the worthy lord of Warwick, as appeareth by the strokes of the great guns in the king's walls of his castle of Bamburgh' [58]. Worcester was a notoriously harsh judge, hated for his ruthlessness, and Grey was duly executed on 10 July.

The war in the north was, at last, over.

Notes:

[1] Hicks M A, 'Edward IV, The Duke of Somerset and Lancastrian Loyalism in the North', Northern History vol. xx p.24

[2] Ibid. p.25

[3] Ross C, 'Edward IV' London 1974 pp.51-52

[4] Hicks op. cit. p.31

[5] Gregory's Chronicle pp.221-223

[6] Hicks op. cit. p.32

[7] Ibid. p.33

[8] Ibid. p.34

[9] *Fabyan's Chronicle* p.683

[10] *Gregory's Chronicle* p.224

[11] *Year Book of Edward IV* p.cviii

[12] Gillingham J, *'The Wars of the Roses'* 1981

[13] *Gregory's Chronicle* p.224

[14] Ibid. p.224

[15] Ibid. p.224

[16] Ibid. p.224

[17] Ibid. p.224

[18] Haigh P A, *'The Military Campaigns of the Wars of the Roses'* 1995

[19] *Gregory's Chronicle* p.224

[20] Boardman A V, *'The Battle of Towton'* 1998

[21] Haigh op. cit. p.80

[22] Brenan op. cit. p.93

[23] Ross op. cit. p.56

[24] Ramsay J H, *'Lancaster and York'* vol. II p.302

[25] *Paston Letters* no.252

[26] Ramsay op. cit. vol. II p.302

[27] Ross op. cit. p.55

[28] Ibid. p.56

[29] *Gregory's Chronicle* p.226

[30] *Fabyan's Chronicle* p.654

[31] *Chronicles of London* ed. C.L. Kingsford Oxford 1905 p.178

[32] Long B, *'The Castles of Northumberland'* 1967 p.76

[33] Lomas op. cit. p.136

[34] Ibid. pp.154-155

[35] Charlesworth D, *'The Battle of Hexham'* 1952 p.62

[36] *Gregory's Chronicle* p.224

[37] Ibid. p.232

[38] Charlesworth op. cit. p.63

[39] *Worcester's Chronicle* p.779

[40] Ramsay op. cit. vol. II 303

[41] Charlesworth op. cit. p.64

[42] Haigh op. cit. p.84

[43] Ramsay op. cit. vol. II p.303n

[44] Ibid. p.303

[45] *Warkworth's Chronicle* p.4

[46] *Fabyan's Chronicle* p.654

[47] *Chronicles of London* p.178

[48] *Fabyan's Chronicle* p.654

[49] *Gregory's Chronicle* p.219

[50] 'Edward' is also listed in an inventory of 1475; the Master of the Ordnance, John Sturgeon, handed into store at Calais, 'divers parcels of the King's ordnance and artillery including a bumbartell called "The Edward"'. See Blackmore 1976 p.33

[51] Bates C, *'History of Northumberland'* p.202

[52] *NCH* vol. 1 p.47

[53] *Worcester's Chronicle* p.280n – the assumption may be based on a misreading of the Latin text: 'Radulfus Gray fugit de Hexham ante bellum inceptum ad castrum Bamburghe et post bellum de Hexham multi ex parte Regis Henrici fugerunt in eodem castro'. It is more probable that the chronicler is describing Grey's flight as the battle opened rather than beforehand.

[54] *NCH* op. cit. p.48

[55] *Warkworth's Chronicle* op. cit. pp.37-39

[56] *NCH* op. cit. p.48.

[57] *Warkworth's Chronicle* op. cit. pp.37-39

[58] *NCH* op. cit. p.49

PART EIGHT

THE LEGACY

With his enemies scattered or killed, King Edward IV appeared to be secure at last. However, after the long struggle against the Lancastrians he was left with a threat within his own faction: his cousin the Earl of Warwick, also known as 'The Kingmaker'. Although Warwick had striven so diligently for the King's cause, he had become the 'Overmighty Subject', a man with an overwhelming sense of his own destiny who expected to be the executive power behind the throne, the master manipulator.

It came as a surprise to Warwick to discover that the King was not so malleable. Although hedonistic, Edward was always formidable. His marriage to *parvenue* Elizabeth Woodville in May 1464 upset Warwick's plan for dynastic union (he had planned that Edward should marry a French princess) and the rise of the Herberts, another ambitious family, widened further the division between the two men. Gradually, the King and his minister separated. His power having been usurped by the new queen's family, Warwick switched his support to George, Duke of Clarence, the King's untrustworthy younger brother and heir. Clarence married Warwick's daughter Isobel in defiance of an express royal edict.

A carefully orchestrated series of disturbances in the North heralded

Warwick's first rising. The King was outmanoeuvred and taken with the Herberts, who were defeated and executed at Edgecote. There followed a partial rapprochement between Warwick and Edward, but he and Clarence were soon implicated in fresh disturbances. Their supporters were scattered at Empingham (or 'Lose-cote field' – so called because the rebel supporters cast away their livery coats as they fled, discarding evidence of the involvement of the Earl and the Duke). Warwick and Clarence were obliged to seek refuge in France where, in the most surprising turn of events in the whole confusion of loyalties, the Earl, aided by the King of France, brokered an agreement with the exiled Margaret of Anjou. To unseat Edward they planned to replace him with the pathetic figure of Margaret's husband Henry VI, presently lodged in the Tower of London, a forgotten and scruffy spectre.

The 'Re-adeption' of Henry VI (whereby he was put back on the throne, undoing the accession of Edward IV) proved to be the masterstroke of the Kingmaker's career. Edward and his younger brother Richard of Gloucester were forced to flee to Burgundy, when John Neville, Lord Montagu, who had stayed aloof from his brother Warwick's earlier treason, now threw in his lot with Warwick and Clarence. For the last time, Henry VI became a puppet king. Whilst Margaret dallied, beset by uncertainty on the continent, the Kingmaker's shaky régime began to unravel.

In 1471, Edward IV and his brother Richard of Gloucester returned from France with a handful of supporters and, after a slow start, raised enough forces to challenge Warwick to battle at Coventry. As a commander, Warwick proved to be no real match for Edward and the final reckoning came on the misty heath at Barnet. A confused and protracted fight ensued, with both Warwick and Montagu perishing in the final rout – the Neville family had fallen.

Margaret now landed in the South West and Edward was obliged to hurry and seek a further trial of arms. In the spring heat a deadly pursuit was conducted until the Lancastrians, led on the field by Somerset's younger brother Edmund, were brought to bay and destroyed at Tewkesbury. Edward of Lancaster, the Queen's son, fell on the field or in the rout; Henry VI was quietly murdered in the Tower, the Lancastrian cause was finally in utter ruin.

Death of Prince Edward

Now was the Yorkist age, the canvas on which Edward and his Queen created splendour that almost rivalled the dazzling display of Burgundy, the most fashionable court in Europe. Clarence was reconciled to his brother before Barnet, but he proved to be troublesome and was disposed of in 1478, drowned in a butt of malmsey according to Shakespeare. Richard of Gloucester remained staunch, ruling Warwick's former great fief of the North from Middleham. The Percy family regained the Earldom of Northumberland in 1470 and Henry Percy, 4th Earl of Northumberland, co-operated with Richard Duke of Gloucester (King Edward's brother) to recover Berwick in 1482. After this date, it remained in English hands.

When the King died suddenly the following year, Richard of Gloucester, aided by the Duke of Buckingham, moved quickly to seize control of the young Edward V, the late King's son. This move was at first welcomed: Edward's mother was a Woodville, and the grasping Woodvilles were universally loathed. Not so welcome was Richard of Gloucester's next move, his usurpation of the crown from his nephew, thus becoming Richard III. As an observer recalled, Richard III was never secure on his throne, having 'one hand always upon his dagger'. Henry Tudor, the forgotten pretender, gained support from the exiled survivors of Lancaster and the remnant of the Woodville faction. Buckingham proved fickle and a botched rebellion soon led to his execution.

*Richard III
at Bosworth*

As we read at the beginning of this book, on 22 August 1485 at Bosworth, Richard III became the last King of England to fall in battle, his ally Percy standing back, preferring expediency to honour. Percy survived to become a servant of Henry VII (the first Tudor king) but was murdered by a mob in York some four years later.

PART NINE

THE BATTLEFIELD TRAIL

The visitor to historic Northumberland is spoiled to a degree, insofar as the topography of the county has been little affected by subsequent development outside the Tyneside conurbation and the rump of the former south-east Northumberland coalfield. It is therefore possible to visit the majority of the historic locations described in this book and to glean an understanding of how they might have looked in the 15th Century.

*The Black Gate
and city walls, Newcastle.*

*The walls and gatehouse
were built after 1247.
The gate was typical of a new
and improved 13th Century
style which
allowed the defenders
flanking fire.*

Your tour begins at **Newcastle,** the principal medieval port on the north-east coast, through which came the bulk of Yorkist supplies and material for the sieges of the Northumbrian castles. Although there are relatively few medieval parts discernable, it is possible to see the Keep of the old castle, one of the finest remaining examples of Norman military architecture, dating from 1172-1177. This is situated near the Quayside, once a thriving industrial hub, now home to the Law Courts and a centre of culture and recreation. It is worth walking to find the Keep, allowing time to walk over the award winning Millennium Bridge to the Baltic and Sage Buildings on the Gateshead side of the River Tyne. The town walls, parts of which remain, were built in the 13th and 14th Centuries; including four magisterial gates, these can be seen not far from the city centre.

Warkworth Castle

The stone castle, which replaced a wooden building on this site, probably dates from the 12th Century, with progressive extensions throughout the Middle Ages.

Leave the city, heading north on the A1 (a dual carriageway of sorts) until you reach Morpeth. Here you quit the larger road for the 'coastal route', north and east from the town via the B1337. This takes you through Widdrington and Broomhill to Amble and thence to **Warkworth**, 'that worm-eaten hold of ragged stone'. The castle is anything but in fact, much of it surviving and in the care of English Heritage. There is a charming riverside walk to the adjacent Hermitage, a romantic oddity that has connections with the Knights Templar. For balmy days there are boats to hire on the river immediately below the castle and plenty of beautiful space for picnics.

From Warkworth, continue to Alnmouth and swing westwards into **Alnwick,** where the great bulk of the castle dominates the town – still very much a Percy seat. The fortress itself is managed by the Percy Estate and was much altered in the 18th Century and again in the 19th Century. It possesses a number of original features and never fails to impress, its sheer bulk and majesty being evidence in stone of 'no king but a Percy'. The visitor today may also wish to visit the outstanding Alnwick Gardens established by the current Duchess. Its fountains and other water features make it the Versailles of Northumberland and it has one of the largest tree houses in the world, which has an excellent and inexpensive restaurant.

Alnwick Castle

Majestic home of the Percy family for generations, the castle at Alnwick has much to offer the visitor.

From Alnwick we follow the B1340 toward the coast, then along minor roads to Dunstan, and we reach finally the picturesque fishing village of Craster. Parking is difficult here, so it is easiest to leave your car in the car park on the right as you enter the village. North of the village along a level shingle strand stands **Dunstanburgh Castle,** still mighty on its dolerite outcrop, 'the fortress of Earl Thomas'. This site, too, is in the care of English Heritage, and is well worth the beautiful walk along the coast to reach it. Craster kippers are world renowned and may be bought from the smokery in the village, which is up the hill in the opposite direction

Once one of the greatest castles of the North, Dunstanburgh dominates a spectacular and lonely stretch of the Northumbrian coastline.

from the road to the castle. From Craster follow the B1339/B1340 as the road hugs the coast, towards Bamburgh.

On your way north, if you have plenty of time, there are regular journeys by boat from Seahouses across to the Farne Islands, once home of St Cuthbert, who died in 687AD. The visit takes about 2½ hours, and includes time on Inner Farne. There are spectacular views of sea bird sanctuaries (puffins, guillemots, kittiwakes) and grey seal colonies.

Lordly **Bamburgh** is perhaps the most impressive of all these great coastal holds – the seat of kings, cradle of the ancient Anglian kingdom of Northumbria, whose rulers, in the Heroic Age, were acknowledged as *Bretwalda, primus inter pares,* of the Saxon kings of England. Before that Bamburgh may have been the 'Joyous Garde' of Sir Thomas Malory's *Morte D'Arthur,* to which Lancelot brought Guinevere. Bamburgh is now in the hands of the Armstrong family and there is a great deal to see inside its stately walls. There are splendid sands for walks and picnics immediately beneath the castle. In the nearby church is the tomb of Florence Nightingale, heroine of the village. From Bamburgh follow the B1342 back to the A1 and proceed north to **Berwick upon Tweed.**

In 1464 Sir Ralph Grey, knowing that he would face execution even if he surrendered, forced Warwick to use the King's artillery against the walls of Bamburgh Castle, much against his will. It became the first ever English castle to fall to artillery fire.

Again, if tide and time allow, it is worth taking a detour to visit Holy Island (Lindisfarne, spiritual home of the illuminated Gospels) as you journey northwards. Berwick, jewel of the English east march, was hotly contended before Richard, Duke of Gloucester finally wrested possession of it from the Scots (whose town it was originally), and it became a *bastide,* a fortified outpost. Most of the magnificent walls are part of the Elizabethan reconstruction, which reduced the *enceinte* from the larger area covered previously. However, traces of the Edwardian walls survive north of the present bastions and the castle once stood on the ground occupied by the main line station; sections of the original wall and Watergate can be traced beyond in the descent to the river Tweed.

And it is the somnolent and romantic twist and flow of the Tweed that we follow inland, first along the A698 and then the minor B6470 to **Norham**, 'the Queen of Border Fortresses'. Here Scott sites the tale of Sir Walter Marmion, during the long Scottish siege of 1318-1320; much of the castle remains and the skeletal massif of the great keep still soars above the broad sweep of the river below. William Turner painted many pictures of Norham Castle between 1797 and 1845, the most famous being *Norham Castle, Sunrise.*

From the village return to the A698 and proceed in a westerly direction to Cornhill on Tweed, where you join the A697, now heading south after a left turn, down towards Wooler. South of that town past Roseden and then just beyond Wooperton is the field of **Hedgeley Moor.** You will come first to the site of **Percy's Leap** on your right, immediately past the village; there are some interpretation boards and a good view of the field from the Lancastrian position. Further south, a mile or so and on your left, standing in a private garden, is **Percy's Cross** (left).

Continue on your southward journey, remaining on the A697 until you reach the B6341 crossroads; here you turn to the right, leaving the main road and head over the high sweep of moorland to Rothbury. From this delightful village you need to head south west along the B6342, through Rothley and Cambo to reach the A696. If you have time, nearby Wallington Hall and its gardens (National Trust) are well worth the visit. Crossing the main road continue on the B6342 as far as the junction with the A68, where you turn left to head south towards Corbridge. To find **Bywell Castle**: at the junction with the A69 follow the A69 towards Newcastle. At the next roundabout turn right (south) back onto the A68 and follow the road (crossing the Tyne) to the next roundabout. Turning left towards Prudhoe on the A695, before you enter Stocksfield turn left onto the B6309 and re-cross the Tyne, then turn left immediately and follow signs to Bywell. Here you can see the old gatehouse (known as the castle) where Henry VI stayed before the Battle of Hexham. It is a private estate which can be visited only by appointment, but merely walking around it gives a fair idea of its history and beauty. From Bywell, retrace your steps back onto the A695 and continue west through Riding Mill towards Hexham, looking for a left hand turning to Dilston Castle, via the B6307 which will be on your left.

Linnels Bridge spans the ravine of Devil's Water It carries a slab with the date of an earlier bridge, built in 1581 to replace the ford.

This takes you past the wildly romantic ruins of Dilston with its association with the doomed 3rd Earl of Derwentwater and the Jacobite cause (that, however, is a different war!). Continue past Dilston and **Swallowship Hill** will soon be on your right. You are approaching the field of the Battle of Hexham from the Yorkist perspective; to glean an idea of the Lancastrian route from Hexham and the pell-mell of the rout, follow the B306 down to Linnels Bridge and proceed into **Hexham.**

As you admire the pleasing market square, think of those whose lifeblood spurted over the cobbles here after the battle. In the market place there are three reminders of the time of the Wars of the Roses: it is framed on one side by the wonderful ancient Abbey, where the body of the executed Duke of Somerset is supposed to lie. On the other is the Moot Hall and behind it the ancient Gaol where those to be executed almost certainly spent their final hours. In the Shambles in the middle of the square is a plaque commemorating the executions of May 1464. This place has something of a grim history as over forty people died here from gunfire in the course of an anti-conscription riot in 1761.

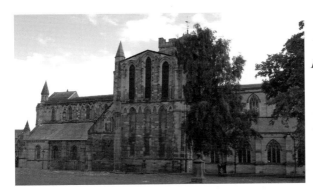

Hexham Abbey, founded by St Wilfrid c.674, became St Andrew, the Parish Church of Hexham after the Dissolution of the Monasteries

Those who wish to study the arms and armour of the period should contemplate a visit either to the **Castle Museum, York** or to the **Royal Armouries in Leeds:** both have some fine survivors from the period. **Micklegate Bar** in York still stands, where numbers of the 'players' (or at least their heads) ended their public careers. The city also possesses a small, somewhat idiosyncratic but charming **Richard III Museum.**

Further afield, **Kelvin Grove Museum in Glasgow** has a superb Milanese field harness from c.1450, precisely the type of armour that the combatants at Hedgeley and Hexham would have worn.

TIMELINE

- 1399: The Lancastrian usurpation; death of Richard II
- 1402: Battle of Homildon
- 1403: Battle of Shrewsbury
- 1415: Battle of Agincourt
- 1420: Treaty of Troyes
- 1422: Death of Henry V
- 1424: Battle of Vernueil
- 1428: Siege of Orleans
- 1435: End of the Anglo-Burgundian Alliance
- 1437: Henry VI comes of age
- 1450: Fall of William de la Pole, Duke of Suffolk
- 1453: Battle of Castillon, end of English hopes in France
- 1453: August, Henry VI has mental breakdown
  The Percy v Neville feud erupts
- 1454: March, York appointed as Protector
- 1454: December, Henry VI recovers
- 1455: February, York resigns as Protector
- 1455: May, First Battle of St Albans
- 1455: November, York re-appointed to the Protectorate
- 1456: February, end of York's second Protectorate
- 1458: March, 'Loveday' at St. Pauls
- 1458: November, putative attempt to kill the Earl of Warwick
- 1459: September, Battle of Blore Heath
- 1459: Oct, the 'Rout of Ludford'
- 1460: June/July, Warwick and March land in Kent
  Battle of Northampton
- 1460: Oct, York recognised heir to Henry VI.
  Edward of Lancaster disinherited.
- 1460: December, Battle of Wakefield
- 1461: February, Battle of Mortimer's Cross
- 1461: February, Second Battle of St Albans
- 1461: March, Earl of March proclaimed Edward IV.
  Battle of Towton.
- 1462: War in Northumberland, Lancastrians hold coastal
  fortresses. Berwick surrenders

- 1463: War in the North splutters on; castles surrender
  Margaret of Anjou flees to France
- 1464: May, battles of Hedgeley Moor and Hexham,
  Montagu created Earl of Northumberland
- 1465: July, capture of Henry VI
- 1469: Warwick plots to overthrow Edward IV
  The Duke of Clarence marries the Earl's daughter
- 1469: July, Battle of Edgecote
- 1469: Edward IV regains control
- 1470: March, Battle of 'Losecote Field' (Empingham)
- 1470: July, Warwick and Clarence in exile in France,
  Warwick comes to an agreement with Margaret of Anjou
- 1470: September, Edward and the Duke of Gloucester
  flee Warwick's coup
- 1471: March, return of Edward IV and Gloucester
- 1471: April, Battle of Barnet
- 1471: May, Battle of Tewkesbury/death of Henry VI,
  Gloucester assumes Warwick's offices as warden, begins
  his tenure in the north
- 1475: July, Edward IV launches French expedition
- 1478: February, killing of the Duke of Clarence
- 1482: Gloucester launches Scottish campaign,
  recovers Berwick and occupies Edinburgh
- 1483: April/June, death of Edward IV, Gloucester seizes
  power, destroys the Woodvilles, executes Lord Hastings,
  assumes the throne as Richard III, Edward V and the Duke of York
  (the Princes in the Tower) are confined
- 1483: October, the Duke of Buckingham's rebellion
- 1484: Richard III rules an uneasy realm
- 1485: August, landing of the Lancastrians under Henry Tudor.
  Battle of Bosworth Field. Death of Richard III
- 1487: June, Battle of Stoke
- 1488: Death of James III of Scotland
- 1491: Perkin Warbeck begins his career as Richard of York
- 1499: Warbeck finally executed
- 1509: Death of Henry VII of England

GLOSSARY

Advowson: the lord's right to appoint an incumbent to a living.

Affinity: a magnate's following, comprising not just his own *vassals* or tenants but his friends and allies.

Annuity: the grant of a pension for life, payable in annual instalments, usually granted by the Crown or magnate.

Attainder: statutory deprivation of one found guilty of treason, forfeiture of all estates, rights and privileges. In the context of the Wars of the Roses, the inevitable consequence of failure or defeat.

Bailey: courtyard of a castle

Banneret: a knight who was entitled to carry his own banner, conferred status over more junior knights, likely to be given a command in battle.

Barbican: outwork defending the entrance to a castle

Bevor: a section of plate armour, worn with the *sallet* form of helmet to provide protection to the neck and lower face.

Bill: a pole arm, a deadly fusion of agricultural implement and spear, with a curved axe-type blade, a spike for thrusting and a hook on the reverse; a formidable weapon in trained hands.

Bombard: a heavy siege gun of the fifteenth century, irregular in calibre but throwing a massive ball, perhaps up to 60lbs in weight.

Bond: an agreement or contract, confirmed by the pledge of cash as a *recognisance* – a surety for the act to be performed or for the refraining from an act, obviously forfeit should the contracting party default on the terms of the bond.

Captain: the officer responsible for a particular place or location but whose authority was limited to his charge.

Chamber: the fiscal aspect or operation of the Royal Household; the management of the Royal accounts as distinguished from the *Exchequer*, then as now the finances of the state as a whole.

Chancery: the executive and administrative function of the Crown.

Chevauchée: a large scale foray aimed at laying waste the territory of an enemy, causing economic damage and belittling the foe, perhaps forcing him to accept battle.

Commission of Oyer & Terminer: from the French, literally to 'hear and determine', the commissioners were Crown appointees charged with investigating acts of treason, felonies (serious offences) and misdemeanours (lesser offences) committed in a particular county or locality.

Constable: the official in charge of a magnate's tenantry who might exercise his office within the lord's residence or with his soldiery in the field.

Crenellation: the form of battlements on a castle's parapet, 'licence to crenellate' being required before a castle could be constructed.

Demesne: a lord or magnate's personal holdings, those occupied and managed by him as opposed to being parcelled out to a tenant or tenants.

Destrier: a warhorse, much prized and of considerable value.

Donjon: keep (of castle)

Enceinte: the circuit of the walls of a defended castle or town.

Escalade: attack, as in an attempt at storming fixed defences such as a castle or town walls, or field defences.

Feudalism: the system of government and land holding introduced into England by William I; the feudal pyramid whereby land was parcelled out to the tenants-in-chief, together with rights attaching thereto, in return for a complex raft of obligations, inherent amongst which was military service for defined periods and duration. The system prevailed all the way down the social scale from sub-tenants to the unfree agrarian poor or *villeins*. 'Bastard Feudalism' is a difficult concept, championed by Stubbs in the 19th Century but revised by MacFarlane subsequently – it embodies the notion of service being undertaken for cash payment rather than as part of a wider obligation.

Fiefdom: a parcel of land, usually substantial, containing a number of *manors* with rights attached.

Fosse: a defensive ditch.

Gorget: a section of plate armour designed to protect the neck area.

Halberd: a form of polearm with a broad axe blade.

Hand and a Half Sword: the knightly sword of the fifteenth century, often known as a 'bastard sword'. Its long, tapering, double-edged blade could be used either for the thrust or the cut.

Harness: full plate armour.

Hobiler(ar): lightly mounted cavalry or mounted infantry, associated with the light horse of the Anglo-Scottish border.

Impeach: to arraign a magnate in front of his peers in Parliament.

Indenture: a form of legally binding agreement, the engrossment of which was, upon completion, cut into two halves along an indentation; an 'employee' or *retainer* could be contracted into service by means of an indenture.

Jack: a form of protective doublet. Stuffed with rags and generally sleeveless, worn by the commons, a more sophisticated form was the *brigandine* which had metal plates sewn between the facing and lining so that only the rivet heads, in decorative patterns, showed through the fabric covering.

Kettle Hat: a form of metal headgear worn by men at arms, with a wide protective brim, similar in appearance to British helmets, 'tin hats', of both world wars.

Lance: a tactical unit built around a knight's following, and could therefore vary in size.

Leaguer: a siege or blockade.

Livery: distinctive coat ('livery coat') worn by the lord's retainers,  bearing his badge, thus the expression 'livery and maintenance'. The retainer was clothed and fed by his employer in return, in effect, for wearing his private uniform (and assuming his private quarrels). The Battle of Empingham or 'Lose-cote Field' refers to the haste with which the panicking rebels cast off the incriminating livery coats of their paymasters Warwick and Clarence.

Manor: a form of landholding, a knightly estate usually comprising the residence of the gentleman, a village or villages, woods, fields, mill(s), wine presses, church etc.

March: a frontier territory, administered by a warden; 'Marcher' lords were those who held lands along the Anglo-Scottish or Welsh borders.

Mark: (currency) 1 mark equalled 13s 4d

Mesnie Knight: one of a lord's household knights, i.e. of his domain or *demesne*

Motte: an earthwork mound on which a castle was built.

Palatinate: lands held by a count palatine, who enjoyed exclusive jurisdiction and extensive, quasi-regal privileges. The Bishops of Durham had the secular office of Counts Palatine for Durham and North Durham (Norhamshire in North Northumberland).

Poleaxe: a polearm, favoured by the gentry for close quarter combat, an axe blade, spear head and a hammer for battering an armoured opponent.

Rondell Dagger: a 15th Century long-bladed knife, carried by all classes, which could be used as a weapon or implement.

Sallet: a 15th Century helmet with a swept neckguard and often fitted with a fixed or moveable visor, worn above the *bevor*.

Tenant-in-chief: magnate who held his lands directly from the Crown, rather than from a superior lord; these were known as sub-tenants.

Vassal: one who holds his land from his feudal superior on terms which involve an obligation of service as a condition of the tenancy.

Vintenar: a breed of NCO in charge of a platoon of twenty men.

Wapentake: a Norse term, literally 'the brandishing of spears in a popular assembly', long established even by 1086 (Domesday). The expression has the same meaning as the Saxon 'Hundred' and refers to main area subdivisions within a given county.

BIBLIOGRAPHY AND SOURCES

(1) A Note on Sources

It is regrettable that none of Newcastle's 15th Century burgesses set out to compile a chronicle of events as the war in the north developed and unfolded; as a consequence we are obliged to rely on sources which are not strictly local. The most significant of these are the London Chronicles, recognised as the most important authorities for the events of the 15th Century.

The common author of both the 'Great Chronicle' and 'The New Chronicle of England' was probably Robert Fabyan (1455-1513), a London draper, Sheriff and then Master of the Drapers Company and a victim of the Woodvilles' rapacity. The Chronicles were written in his later years and the events in the North occurred when he was still a boy.

These London Chronicles were penned by metropolitan writers for a specific audience; the views expressed tend therefore to be somewhat parochial and, given the width of the North/South divide, it is not surprising if regional events receive lesser prominence. The north was culturally and geographically remote; its inhabitants were neither liked nor understood. Fabyan misses out Hedgeley Moor altogether and provides only a cursory account of Hexham.

The War in the North features briefly in the 'Vitellius Chronicle', but the 'Brief Latin Chronicle', is more informed about the opening stages. The 'Brief Notes' written at Ely, essentially a journal of news items, is very useful for the events of 1462. The 'Short English Chronicle', probably written c.1465, is also most helpful.

Nonetheless, events in the North during the early years of Edward IV are poorly served by the chroniclers. One of the best is Gregory's Chronicle, written by an author who was a member of the London Skinners Company and mayor from 1451 to his death in 1467. His work covers a thirty year period, from 1440-1470, so it follows that he was not the sole author. His narrative is the fullest for the years 1461-1454 as far as the North is concerned and he provides us with the most comprehensive list of those executed after Hexham. He was not, of course, a northerner, nor, as far as we are aware, had he ever visited the region.

William Worcester, (or Botoner, his mother's maiden name), was born in Bristol in 1415. As secretary to Sir John Fastolf he was the author of at least some of the Paston correspondence; latterly he resided in London where he died in the early 1480s. His work 'Annales Rerum Anglicarum' was compiled during his time in the metropolis and he seems to have drawn on the London Chronicles for the earlier years. He is good on events in the north and apparently wrote a fine account of Hexham but the page, frustratingly, is missing from the surviving manuscript!

One of the chroniclers, John Warkworth (d.1500), was a Northumbrian, a Fellow of Merton College (1446) and Principal of Neville Inn (1453). He acted as chaplain to William Grey, Bishop of Ely, through whose patronage he was appointed Master of Peterhouse. He probably finished his work around 1482 and he is well informed on the rebellion of 'Robin of Redesdale' in 1469 and on the events of 1470-1471. His coverage of the earlier years, however, is rather meagre.

Bibliography

Primary Sources

Calendar of State Papers and Manuscripts existing in the Archives and Collections of Milan ed. and transl. Hinds A B, 1912

Chastellain G, *Chronique des Derniers Ducs de Bourgoyne* in Pantheon Literaire iv.

Chronicles of London ed. Kingsford C L, Oxford 1905

Hall E, *The Union of the Two Noble and Illustre Famelies of Lancastre and York* 1548

Warkworth J, *A Chronicle of the First Thirteen Years of the Reign of Edward IV 1461-1474,* ed. Halliwell J O C S, Old Series X 1839.

Fabyan R, *The New Chronicles of England and France,* ed. Ellis H, London 1809

Short English Chronicle, ed. Gairdner J C S, New Series xxviii 1880

Talhoffer H, *Manual of Swordfighting,* transl. & ed. Rector M, facsimile edn. 2000

The Year Book de Termino Paschae 4 Edward IV, in Priory of Hexham, S.S. 1 1864

Gregory W, *Chronicle of London' in Historical Collections of a Citizen of London in the Fifteenth Century,* ed. Gairdner J C S, New Series xvii 1876

William of Worcester, *Annales Rerum Anglicarum in Liber Niger Scaccarii,* ed. Hearne J, 2vols. Oxford 1728

Registrum Abbatis Johannis Whethamstede, 1872. ed. Riley H T

Secondary Sources

Archibald E H H, *The Wooden Fighting Ship,* London 1968

Bain J ed. *Calendar of Documents relating to Scotland 1108-1509, 1881-1884; Calendar of Border papers vols. i and ii 1894*

Barbour R, *The Knight and Chivalry,* London 1974

Bartlett C, *The English Longbowman 1313-1515,* England 1995

Bates C J, *History of Northumberland,* London 1895

Bennet M, *The Battle of Bosworth,* New York 1985

Blackmore H L, *The Armouries of the Tower of London – Ordnance,* HMSO 1976

Blair C, *European Armour,* London 1958

Boardman A V, *The Battle of Towton,* England 1994

Boardman A V, *The Medieval Soldier in the Wars of the Roses,* London 1998

Brenan G, *The House of Percy,* 2 vols. England 1898

Burne, Colonel A H, *Battlefields of England,* London 1950

Burne Colonel A H, *More Battlefields of England,* London 1952

Charlesworth D, *Northumberland in the Early Years of Edward IV,* Archaeologia Aeliana 4th Series 1953

Charlesworth D, *The Battle of Hexham,* Archaeologia Aeliana 4th Series 1952

Ducklin K & Waller J, *Sword Fighting,* London 2001

Gillingham J, *The Wars of the Roses,* London 1981

Goodman A, *The Wars of the Roses*, London 1981

Gravett C, *Medieval Siege Warfare*, England 1990

Griffiths R A, *Local Rivalries and National Politics: The Percies, the Nevilles and the Duke of Exeter 1452 -1455*, Speculum vol. xliii 1968 p.589

Griffiths R A, *The Reign of King Henry VI*, London 1981

Haigh P A, *The Battle of Wakefield*, England 1996

Haigh P A, *The Military Campaigns of the Wars of the Roses*, London 1995

Hammond P W, *The Battles of Barnet and Tewkesbury*, New York 1990

Hammond P W, Sutton A, *Richard III – The Road to Bosworth Field*, London 1985

Hepple L W, *A History of Northumberland and Newcastle upon Tyne*, London 1976

Hicks M A, *Edward IV, The Duke of Somerset and Lancastrian Loyalism in the North*, Northern History Vol xx.

James M E, *The Murder at Coxlodge on 28th April, 1489*, Durham University Journal vvii 1965 p.80

Keegan J, *The Face of Battle*, London 1976

Keen M, *English Society in the Later Middle Ages 1348-1500*, England 1990

Keen M, *Medieval Warfare – a History*, Oxford 1999

Murray K P, *Warwick The Kingmaker*, New York 1957

Murray K P, *Richard III*, New York

Jones M K, *Bosworth 1485 – The Psychology of a Battle*, England 2002

Lander J R, *The Wars of the Roses*, London 1990

Lomas R, *Northumberland – County of Conflict*, East Lothian 1996

Lomas R, *North-East England in the Middle Ages*, Edinburgh 1992

Long B, *The Castles of Northumberland*, Newcastle upon Tyne 1967

Lynch M, *A New History of Scotland*, London 1991

McFarlane K B, *The Nobility of Late Medieval England*, Oxford 1975

McFarlane K B, *England in the Fifteenth Century*, ed. G.L. Harris 1981

Meade D M, *The Medieval Church in England*, England 1988.

Mortimer I, *The Greatest Traitor*, London 2003

Neillands R, *The Hundred Years War*, London 1990

Neillands R, *The Wars of the Roses*, London 1992

Nicolle D, *Medieval Warfare Source Book*, London 1999

Norman A V B, Pottinger D, *English Weapons and Warfare 1449-1660*, London 1966

Oakeshott R E, *A Knight and his Weapons*, London 1964

Oman C, *The Art of War in the Middle Ages*, vol. II London 1924

Pevsner N, Richmond I, *Northumberland*, 2nd ed London 1996

Pollard A J, *Percies, Nevilles and the Wars of the Roses*, History Today, September 1992

Pollard A J, *Characteristics of the Fifteenth Century North, in Government, Religion and Society in Northern England 1000-1700*, ed. Appleby C and Dalton P, England 1977

Pollard A J, *The Wars of the Roses*, England 1988

Prestwich M, *Armies and Warfare in the Middle Ages*, London 1996

Ramsay J H, *Lancaster and York*, 2 Vols. Oxford 1892

Ridpath G, *The Border History of England and Scotland,* Berwick upon Tweed 1776

Rogers H C B, *Artillery Through the Ages*, London 1971

Rose A, *Kings in the North*, London 2002

Ross C, *Wars of the Roses,* London 1976

Ross C, *Edward IV*, London 1974

Ross C, *Richard III*, London 1981

Rowse A L, *Bosworth Field and the War of the Roses*, London 1966

Runciman S, *The Fall of Constantinople*, England 1965

Sadler D J, *Battle for Northumbria*, England 1988

Sadler D J, *War in the North – The Wars of the Roses in the North East of England 1461-1464*, England 2000

Sadler D J, *Border Fury – The Three Hundred Years War*, England 2004

Seward D, *Henry V as Warlord*, London 1987

Seward D, *Richard III – England's Black Legend*, England 1983

Seward D, *The Wars of the Roses*, London 1995

Seymour W, *Battles in Britain*, Vol I London 1989

Smurthwaite D, *Battlefields of Britain*, London 1984

Storey R L, *End of the House of Lancaster*, London 1966

Thrupp S L, *The Problem of Replacement Rates in Late Medieval English Population*, ECHR 2nd Series 1965-1966

Weaver T W, *A Comprehensive Guide to Northumberland*, Newcastle upon Tyne 1863

Tough D L W, *The Last Years of a Frontier*, Oxford 1928

Trevelyan G M, *A History of England*, London 1926

Wagner, Heiss S, *Medieval Sword and Shield*, California 2003

Warner P, *Sieges of the Middle Ages*, London 1968

Watson G, *The Border Reivers*, Newcastle upon Tyne 1974

Weiss H, *A Power in the North? The Percies in the Fifteenth Century*, The Historical Journal 19.2 1965 pp.501-509

Wise T, *Medieval Heraldry*, England 1980

Wise T, *The Wars of the Roses*, London 1983

Woolgar C M, *The Great Household in late Medieval England*, London 1999